To Amy, Steve, &

with Love

Matthew & Bjorn

P9-DFT-669

BELIEVING
IT ALL

Also by Marc Parent

TURNING STONES

BELIEVING
IT ALL

WHAT MY CHILDREN
TAUGHT ME ABOUT TROUT FISHING,
JELLY TOAST, AND LIFE

MARC PARENT

LITTLE, BROWN AND COMPANY
BOSTON NEW YORK LONDON

FIRST EDITION

THE AUTHOR IS GRATEFUL FOR PERMISSION TO INCLUDE THE FOLLOWING PREVIOUSLY COPYRIGHTED MATERIAL : LYRICS FROM "IN MEMORY OF MY HEART." WRITTEN BY BUDDY MILLER AND JULIE MILLER COPYRIGHT © 2000. PUBLISHED BY BUGHOUSE / MUSIC OF WINDSWEPT, TINKIE TUNES, AND MARTHA ROAD MUSIC (ASCAP). ADMINISTERED BY BUG. ALL RIGHTS RESERVED. USED BY PERMISSION.

LIBRARY OF CONGRESS CATALOGING-IN-PUBLICATION DATA

PARENT, MARC.

BELIEVING IT ALL : WHAT MY CHILDREN TAUGHT ME ABOUT TROUT FISHING, JELLY TOAST, AND LIFE / MARC PARENT — 1ST ED.

P. CM.

ISBN 0-316-69015-5

I. PARENT AND CHILD — MISCELLANEA. I. TITLE.

HQ755.85 .P352 2001

306.874 — DC21

00-048790

10 9 8 7 6 5 4 3 2 1

Q-FF

TEXT DESIGN BY MERYL SUSSMAN LEVAVI/DIGITEXT

PRINTED IN THE UNITED STATES OF AMERICA

For Casey and Owen

And for Mitchell

CONTENTS

[vii]

BELIEVING
IT ALL

PEDAL STEEL

There's a country station on. The sound is low. Except for an occasional *my heart breaks . . .* or *still miss her . . .* the soft drone of a pedal steel is all that comes through. I like the sound of it to distract from the clicking of my fingers against these keys. I'm in a small, renovated room of an old barn. A fan sits in the far corner, blowing air over a heater to keep the warmth from crowding against the ceiling. It's the last weekend of February — one of the warmest on record — and it seems the leaves coaxed from their buds by this false spring might have to fight to make it to September.

I live with my family in an old farmhouse in a place called Cherry Valley. Just before seven each morning, my wife, Susan, drives off to spend the day with other people's children. She's a fifth-grade teacher. While she's gone, I spend the long, quiet days with our two sons. In the evening, I walk up to this barn and write down the things they've taught me.

My oldest is three. My youngest is nearly one. It's not their intention to teach me. It's my intention to learn from them.

The classroom is a simple twelve acres. It's wooded, mostly — stands of cedar freckled with an occasional struggling maple and then giving way to a towering forest of old-growth poplar. Like a collapsing moss-covered spine down the middle of the property, a wide stone wall curves and dips back and over a stream that ranges from brook to creek to small river depending on the weather and the season. There's deer, raccoon, ambling groups of turkey, grouse that flush like Chinese rockets, an occasional bear, blankets of violets and hairy vines of poison ivy, luna moths and bees the size of crab apples. The wide-open parcels of adjacent lands haven't yet fallen prey to what's been heralded in most parts of the country as progress. Remnant logging roads lead straight back into a cradle of the Kittatinny Mountains, where they fade, disappear, and come magically back until they meet on a high ridge with the Appalachian Trail.

The ridge is visible from the bedroom windows of our weathered clapboard house. Built up from its stone foundation at the turn of the last century, a chiseled rock fireplace added in the fifties, the wraparound porch ripped off in the mid-seventies, a covered slate patio added in the late eighties, the structure still maintains the feel its builders must have intended those many years ago — not merely that of a house but of a home. Of all the rooms, the kitchen is the largest.

The setting here is very much like that of my childhood. I was raised in the country. I was a country kid like any other, with a pressed-wood dresser full of hand-me-down shirts in all the colors of your better bass lures, a belly half-full of green apples and river water, bangs too long, socks pulled high under long pants on the hottest day of summer, and the only thing better than lighting a match off the fly of your jeans was spending the whole afternoon and a whole box trying to make it look natural. I was a spear whittler, pellet shooter, bridge jumper, smoke bomber, farmhouse-dog-at-the-road fighter like they all are. Friends on mini-bikes with dirt on their cheeks and pockets full of ball bearings to lay on the tracks — *Got your steelies?* we'd shout back and forth, cupping our crotches, falling over with laughter. *Hey, man — you gonna put your balls on the tracks?* — hooting like sailors until the train smashed them into thin steel disks that would warm our pockets on the way home.

Even as a boy, I hoped that the setting of my childhood might still exist someday for my own children. That there would be enough worms in the ground for them to make a decent stew to go with the mud pie. I hoped the stars would burn as bright and the rivers run as furiously in the spring, that there would still be hatchets for sale at department stores and enough young saplings so you could cut down a few just to yell, *Tim-ber*.

I hoped for a setting that would broaden their minds like a good classroom. A welcoming and forgiving place. A place where they could let down their guard and make mistakes on the way to getting things right. One overflowing with props to engage the senses and provoke the mind — a dizzying flow of dying things and things being born, some falling down and others springing up, some killed, some mended. A place that challenged without intimidating.

Comforted without pacifying. A place with ice cream in the freezer. Crayon marks on the walls. An occasional fresh loaf of bread on the counter. Sharp kitchen knives. Firewood that started easily. And at least one carpeted room with a space cleared for wrestling.

This is that kind of place.

The moment my first son was born, I looked close into his puckered face and caught in his eyes a glimpse of infinity. It was still fresh. Looking in, I had the feeling I was standing at the edge of something huge — a mystery as vast and subtle as anything in Nature. I followed him into the nursery, where he was joined by twelve other newborns whose eyes held the same power. They were mostly quiet, their limbs arcing randomly in the air. With eyes too new to look out, they were still looking in and drawing me with them, dwarfing my lifetime of experience in the awesome force of their inward gaze. No teaching could ever approach the sensible wisdom contained in those dark orbs, before the formation of irises, when the color of all eyes is only darkness — an absence of everything but the essential and real. It was impossible to imagine that the doctors, the nurses, the strangers in the elevator, the people in their cars going to parties, going to movies, going to therapy, going to church — that we all might have once come into the world with eyes that held such unencumbered truth. And that over the years we could have lost so much of it.

One of the first things I came to believe after my first son's arrival was that my life up to that point had been a long pe-

riod of forgetting. With his birth came an invitation to remember. This new spirit, not yet limited by language or
shaped by experience, still connected to the womb's darkness, was a bridge into the essence of patience and waiting
and longing to be. In his simple reflexes were all the deepest
territories from rage to love — the widest spectrum of sen-
sibility, an ageless, universal wisdom that we all sprang
from, one that gets covered over with the putting on of
years, so much so that by the time we've reached adulthood,
it's not what we've learned that makes us who we are, it's
what we've forgotten. Moving to the rhythm of a child is a
dance of remembrance, tracing us back to the wholeness we
once held as a reflex.

What if there are actually answers to some of the biggest
questions in life? I used to think about the kind of person
who might be able to give me those answers — someone
much older, someone wiser, with smoky eyes and a gravelly
voice. I used to imagine the person emerging on the horizon
just when I had given up on ever finding the true path and
then suddenly walking up and handing me everything —
stunning insights into the deepest regions of love, rage,
kindness, cruelty, forgiveness, gratitude, living, dying, holding on, and, finally, letting go. I never thought that I might
know the ones who could unlock these mysteries. That I
might already be living with them. I might be wiping their
noses and begging them to keep the bathwater in the tub. I
never thought that I might lean in to hear the answers only
to discover that they are revealed without the utterance of a

single word — revealed without warning — given only once, and usually hidden beneath the roar of everyday living. I never thought I would have to crouch down for the lessons. I never thought the greatest teacher I could ever hope to discover was a child.

The truth is, I haven't come up with any of this. I've only written down the things my children have shown me. The words are mine. The wisdom is theirs. A child only knows the things that are true. Words can lie but children never do.

The lessons began immediately.

THE SQUIRREL

The only thing better than a day like this is a whole week of days like this. The meadowlarks and juncos seem to think so too as they warble and hop through the trees along the road we're walking. A March day so crisp the air seems to crack as you walk through it. Casey in a large green stroller built to accommodate a father's stride and much heavier than other strollers because, except for the hubs, it's all metal. Owen in a backpack. We're all very much to ourselves — the three of us strapped together in body yet separate in mind. Even though I'm the engine running this train, my head flies effortlessly to worlds away.

We're on Lower Cherry Valley Road. There is no Upper Cherry Valley Road. There's no road above this one and the road on the other side of Cherry Valley is called, just, Cherry Valley. I haven't seen a cherry tree since we moved here. Our neighbor, who grew up on this road, remembers when it was made out of dirt and you could sit cross-legged in the middle to sing songs and slap hands with friends. Despite the pavement, the feel remains. As it thinly winds its way through the valley, you can almost imagine a time when there must have been cherries.

We do this walk several times a week. There is no destination. The itinerary is straight ahead until I get tired or someone starts to cry uncontrollably. It's a way for the three of us to load ourselves up with the feel of the landscape. The only difference between a place to live and a holy land is the number of footsteps you've put into the ground. To know a place is to love a place and to know a place is to have walked it. I want to love this place. I want the swell in the horizon to burn its outline across my chest. I want to look out over the fields in the middle of the night with my head on a pillow and my eyes closed. I want to wear this place in my bones. I want to smell it in my wife's hair and see it reflected in Casey and Owen's eyes. But first, I have to walk it.

Casey didn't trust the country initially. The unfamiliar crunch of poplar leaves and the twigs whipping his busy legs as I hauled him through the forest made him cry for home, or for the lawn, before we ever got far. At his age, the whole place was a damn uncertainty. The cry of circling Cooper's hawks, their sound designed by nature to make a rabbit betray itself in a run through the field, was also quite good at getting a child's bottom jaw to jut out over his top lip. His small eyes cursed the sound as he looked up into the full sun. I tried everything to warm him to our country home, but nothing could compete with his longing for the cramped apartment and noisy New York City streets we'd left behind. No circling Cooper's hawk could better the dirty, one-footed pigeons flipping too-large crusts of pizza across the cobblestone playgrounds he knew so well. The city had an unbreakable grip on his affection, it seemed. For the past three years, it was all he'd known. It was where he'd walked.

Slowly, this place is catching up. I watch with relief, as the fall of each step melts his distrust of this valley, these roads, this simple farmhouse from which he and his younger brother will weave a childhood.

Owen falls asleep quickly in the rhythmic bump of my gait. Casey leans forward against the front rail and retells himself a story we'd read that morning. I can make out an occasional word when his voice goes into a high inflection with a character's surprise or delight. The occasional phrases narrate our passage through the valley. *"Here I am," said the west wind . . . and blew and blew and blew. . . . "This is my secret place," said the lion. . . . "Help, help!" cried the old mouse. . . .*

I glance up the road. Trees on either side look as though they're waiting to cross. Limb tops lean together, mingling their twigs high above. About a quarter mile up, there's something lying on the road, yellow double lines leading to a small, dark lump in the middle. Casey sees it as we close in on a hundred yards or so.

"What is it?" he asks. I know what it is.

"Let's go see," I say.

We move forward quietly. The narration has stopped.

Just the trees clicking their sticks over us as we come to a stop in front of —

"A squirrel," he says reverently. Dead but completely intact, which makes me think it may have somehow fallen from a branch rather than been hit by a car. We watch for a moment. Besides the fact that it's not moving, the only thing that gives it away as dead is the right eye, which hangs slightly from its socket and is shriveled like a small dry raisin. Welcome to the country. The body is fresh. Farmers and pathologists will tell you: eyes are always the first to go. We look a little longer.

"What?" Casey suddenly demands, as if I've said something. He wants an explanation — why the squirrel isn't acting like the ones we watch in our woods.

"He's not moving, is he?"

"Why?" he asks quickly.

"Well, . . . maybe he's tired," I say, surprised that my first reaction is to explain it away as something other than death.

"What?" Casey asks, knowing there's more to this than garden-variety fatigue. The eye is the give-away. He's old enough to know that no matter how tired you get, eyes don't fall out and dry into raisins.

Like a drunken uncle who crashes through the screen door at suppertime, Mother Nature doesn't soften her demeanor to suit young eyes. One of my favorite memories of growing up in the skillet-flat middle of Wisconsin was watching my father awkwardly skate around an explanation as several dozen young cattle madly humped one another. I only remember him saying something about how "fond" they were of each other. From a child's perspective, that kind of fondness looks more like an all-out war.

"What, Daddy — what?"

It occurs to me that this could be Casey's first real consideration of death. I feel the sudden weight of this and want to say just the right thing. I want to say some wise, fatherly sort of thing. But there's no time to come up with it. Despite the cool air, the sun is warm on the back of my neck. A light sweat has broken over my forehead. I unzip the collar of my jacket. Owen wakes because we've stopped walking. He peers over my shoulder at the squirrel.

"Casey," I say, "that squirrel is dead."

"That squirrel is *dead,*" he mumbles back to himself.

An honest start. I wait to see if he takes it further or if that's enough for now.

"Daddy, that squirrel is *dead,*" he says, dragging the word out as he does with all new words.

"That's right, Case."

"But why is he *dead*?"

Owen pushes up in the backpack for a better look. He reaches around and points at the squirrel. "Huh," he says.

"*Why,* Dad?" Casey asks.

"Maybe a car hit him."

"Maybe a car hit him," he mumbles back.

"Or he might've fallen out of a tree," I say. Casey looks to the branches above us, squinting against the sun. With my hand, I pantomime a squirrel slipping and falling to the road. Casey returns his gaze to the squirrel.

"I want to look at it," he says, and I know what this

means. I lift him out of the stroller so he can crouch down close to it. With his chin at his knees, he slowly tips his head from side to side. I hear him breathing through his nostrils. Then he straightens his neck to look up the road, thinking. He stands. This could be the end of it. But then he drops the big one.

"Daddy, what is *dead* mean?"

And I'm suddenly neck-deep in the kind of solemn moment you anticipate even before having children. The sun beating down on a country road, nothing but the sound of the breeze in your ears, a small dead animal at your feet, and your child looks up and asks you to define one of life's greatest mysteries. You end up having to answer the question for yourself as much as for your child. With every breath, Casey has me test the beliefs, principles, and myths I've held up to life's uncertainties. And if you can break a mystery like death into chunks that fit into the mind of a three-year-old, you've most likely uncovered the core of what really matters.

Casey's eyes look trustingly to mine. In the breeze, his bangs swing back and forth across his forehead. My mind races through possible approaches. Whatever I decide to say will be gospel. It will be The Way It Is, until he archives everything I've ever told him to form his own view of the world — every generation trying to reach a little higher than the last. I give it a try and, for the first time, the sound of my voice is that of a real father's.

"Casey, . . ."

"What?" he says impatiently.

"The squirrel's body is here for us to look at, but the thing that made that squirrel jump and run, the thing that made his tail flicker up and down and wiggle back and forth . . . that isn't there anymore. Because he's dead.

"Remember when the doctor listened to your heart?" He stares up, too focused to nod. "And then you listened to *my* heart? Remember? . . . What did my heart say to you? . . . *duh-dun, duh-dun, duh-dun, duh-dun* . . . remember that?" His eyes are narrowed now. Very serious. "Well, that squirrel has a heart too. Just like you and me. But his heart isn't talking anymore. When your heart says everything it needs to say, when it's all done, it stops talking . . . and when your heart stops talking, you die. Some hearts talk for a long time before they're finished. Other hearts say what they need to say very quickly. And when they finish, they die. Your body stays here but the thing that makes you jump and run, the thing that makes goose bumps — the thing that gives hugs and kisses, that goes away. The squirrel's body is right here, but the squirrel doesn't live in it anymore. He's gone."

"Because he doesn't *live* in it anymore," Casey mumbles back, crouching down again for a close look.

"That's right."

"He doesn't *live* in it anymore," he mutters again, completely absorbed.

I can see his wheels turning. His eyes are filled with speculation. He examines the body with the obsessive focus of a child: instant, complete, fleeting. I am grateful to be with him for this, to see it sinking in. A three-year-old doesn't wait until you get home from work to ask you about a dead squirrel. Three-year-olds live in the moment. I crouch down with him. Owen strains for a better look.

"That squirrel doesn't *live* there anymore because he's *dead*."

"That's right, Case."

We watch a little longer. The sun's warmth has quieted the birds. Owen, standing in his backpack, points again. "Huh," he says. I feel as though I've turned a fast curve into a safe double. I've done right by a difficult, important question. The three of us consider the squirrel in silence. The veneration in the air is palpable. For a moment, the world seems just a bit clearer.

Then Casey looks up, smiling, as he knocks me off the holy golden throne I've just climbed onto. "We can kick it?" he asks cheerfully.

And even as I'm thrown, I feel the wisdom of his irreverence. The message, one of his earliest, will set the ground rules for all the rest: no matter who you are or what you're talking about, never lose sight of the bigger picture, and even when the subject is serious, never take yourself too seriously.

"Well...," I say after a moment. "I guess so... yeah, I guess you can kick it." He does, and Owen lets out a hearty laugh. The squirrel tumbles off the road and is lost in the tall grass.

THE OLD MAN

PART ONE

The man has to be in his seventies, but it's hard to tell. He could be older. A full head of white hair, and looking like he just stepped out of an Orvis fly-fishing catalog. An outdoorsman. Red wool hunting jacket. Red plaid shirt. Redwing boots. He stops his blue Pontiac in the middle of the road and walks right up the lawn to where I'm standing with the boys.

"How are you, Marc?" he asks as if we've known each other for years. I can almost feel the impact of his smile. "Good to see ya. Dick." He shakes my hand and leans down to the boys, who are beaming up at him. "And this must be little Casey and Owen."

"I'm not little," Casey shoots back. "But *he* is little," he says, pointing at Owen.

The old man lets out a long laugh, revealing the majority of his teeth. "Okay, you betcha, big fella. Oh boy," he says looking back at me, "Those sure are some good fellas all right."

"They're good boys," I say.

"Oh, sure they are. Right, little Owen?" he says with another good laugh. "You betcha. Sure. Okay." I'm just about to ask how he knows our names when his voice goes low and serious. "Hey, I put your trash cans up by the house. You never can be too safe about that."

We spent the weekdays in the city when we first bought the house. Trash day was Wednesday, so the cans would spend the week by the road. Except for the last few weeks, when they had been placed neatly onto our porch. The mystery had been driving us crazy.

"Somebody sees them by the road, and the next thing you know, they're in your house," he says, eyebrows reaching into his perfect line of white hair.

"Well, thanks a lot," I say. "We've been wondering who the heck was bringing them up."

"Why, sure. I'll put them up for ya. Oh, you bet. Till you get up here full-time. You can never be too safe. Better that than sorry. Okay, then."

"You live here?" I ask.

"Take care of the property up the way. Grew up here my whole life. Oh, it's changed though. Sure. And not always for the better."

Casey walks up and takes a hold of his finger. "I want to show you something," he says, but he really just wants Dick to himself.

"Oh, not today, big fella," he says with another long, toothy laugh. "I gotta get to the doctor's." He looks at me again with the serious climbing eyebrows. "Spider bite that won't heal up. I was out in the field and — *bang* — got me right on the leg. Oh, you bet. Been seeing the doctor *four years* now. Sure. A terrible thing." Then he laughs and ruffles Casey's hair. "So you boys better stay away from those spiders! Okay, then. Good to meet you, Marc. You come by with the boys sometime. I'm up the road when it's nice out. Sure. We'll see ya."

We watch him climb into the blue Pontiac and rumble away. For some reason, I'm unsettled about an impeccable looking old man with a four-year-old spider bite. The Pontiac disappears behind a hill. I look down at the boys. The old man is gone, but they're still waving and smiling back to their molars. Not unsettled in the least.

THE GAME

Two to four players. Each player has a tree with ten cherries and an empty bucket. A spinner in the middle tells you to pluck one, two, three, or four cherries from your tree and put them in your bucket. If the spinner lands on the puppy or the bird, you have to take two cherries out of your bucket and put them back on your tree. If the spinner lands on the pile of cherries, you have to dump your bucket out and start over again. The first one to get all the cherries from the tree to the bucket *wins*.

Unless you play with a three-year-old and an eleven-month-old, in which case, there is no such thing as winning.

I spotted the game as I passed through the toy department on a milk and banana run at the supermarket. It's an old game. I had it as a kid. I used to love *winning* this game. I don't remember a time when I played it just to move the bright red cherries around.

I expose the board and the boys are awestruck. So many cherries. All so red. All so candylike and rolling merrily in the box top as I set up the game. There are forty of them. The boys reach in and carefully roil their twenty fingers through the pile. Their bodies shake with excitement. Two cherries for each finger.

I put the buckets in the holders, get the spinner turning freely, and start putting cherries on the trees. I can hardly wait to get them playing. *They'll love this game once we get started,* I think. The satisfaction of plucking a tree bare. The beauty of a full bucket. The thrill of yelling, *Hi Ho! Cherry-O,* into the long faces of your opponents.

"Help me put the cherries on the trees," I say. Casey puts one on and then begins to put the rest into the buckets. Owen gets one in his mouth. "On the trees, guys — on the trees," I say. Casey gets two more on his tree and starts to line the rest around the spinner. Owen opens his mouth and calmly lowers his head into the pile. Casey hits the spinner and the cherries fly to the floor. "Go pick them up now," I say, lifting Owen's head and pulling his jaw open. Wet cherries drip from his mouth. Casey lifts two fistfuls above his head and lets them fall to the board in a cherry downpour. Owen thinks this is a super idea. He lifts cherries above his head and drops them into his shirt collar and the cuffs of his jeans. He eats another one.

"Okay — back up, guys," I say sternly. "Back up." They do. Casey lets out a little growl. Owen's bottom lip shoots out. "This is a really fun game, you guys," I say. "C'mon, just let me set it up. It'll be fun. You're gonna love it once I show you how to play."

I give Casey a quick rundown on the game. I'll play for Owen with his occasional input and he'll stay interested in the heat of competition. Standing away from the table, they're both sullen as they watch me load ten cherries onto each tree. Their interest returns when I show them how to whirl the spinner and let them practice.

We start. My first spin lands on the puppy — two out of the bucket and back to the tree. My bucket is empty so I can't do anything. Casey spins. It stops on the puppy again. Nothing. (See how fun?) Owen hits the spinner, knocking all of his cherries and most of mine to the floor. This gets a big laugh. I pick up the cherries, glancing at the two kids on the game box who are playing so nicely with their tidy-looking mother. I'm in the same sweatshirt I wore the day before. Owen slept in his jeans.

Soon we're into the rhythm of a real game. Casey understands. Owen is happy, when it's his turn, just to press flesh to a cherry. We play a fair and consistent round and Casey empties his tree first. He wins. *"You win!"* I say. *"You filled your bucket!"* He seems pleased.

"We can do it again?" he asks.

"Sure," I say.

They stand back while I reload the trees. Casey spins first. Gets the puppy.

"I win!!" he screams.

Owen slaps the board and thirty cherries hop from their hold and roll across the table. See how fun?

I make a few more attempts to right the course of the game, but soon we're hauling cherries in and out of buckets with no rhyme or reason. They load handfuls of cherries into dump trucks and drive them around the carpet. Owen walks into a corner to whirl the spinner. Casey stacks the buckets end to end and crashes a plane into them.

And that's how you play Hi Ho! Cherry-O.

I watch them float with joy and think about how there really was a time when it was all about how you played the game. I don't remember ever playing Hi Ho! Cherry-O, I only remember trying to win it.

We play a lot of cards now. The current favorite is called "Red Card, Black Card." The game is played with a standard deck of cards. Each player starts with a glass of chocolate milk. The cards are split among the players and then turned over one at a time. Red cards in the red pile, black cards in the black pile. The game ends when any one of the players finishes his chocolate milk or gets tired of playing.

Another game they like is called "Number Card, Face Card." Each player starts with a piece of jelly toast. But you get the picture.

THE GIFT

The barn feels like an old granddad, its gray oak timbers and silver planks somehow more knowing than I could ever be. It's night. The wind whistles hard through the slats. In my room, the radio is low — pedal steel whining like it's coming from the next county . . . *tears come faster . . . nights grow longer* . . . as I sit here thinking about my first steps into fatherhood. Our apartment in the city with Casey when he was just two days old. So peaceful in the glow of our new child. Susan wiping the tears from her cheeks as she held him. So relieved to be out of the hospital. So secure in the feeling that we'd crossed through the fire, that everything was fine, that we'd made it.

Then a single incident that changed everything. An event that began a spiritual reckoning on a level that distilled the complexity of life down to the few things you'd surround with your own blood to save.

Casey stopped breathing twenty minutes after Susan and I brought him home from the maternity floor. She was in the living room in a new black rocker we'd bought in his honor a week earlier. I had just laid him at the foot of our bed and was reaching for a diaper when his throat mysteriously closed up and his small face spun into a silent grimace.

As I leaned down to him, it was plain to see he was in a struggle, but newborns seem to be struggling with and against everything in the first few days. I'd seen the shirt collar against his chin set off a battle of random grimaces and grunts, one hand pushing and the other grasping at the air. But this was different. His body was tight. He didn't move. The sudden onset caught me so off guard, I felt more confused than horrified.

Susan came running before I could call out to her. His color changed from dark red to purple as he strained for breath under an enormous invisible weight.

"He's not breathing," she said immediately. The severity in her voice was unnerving; it made the looming tragedy suddenly inescapable.

"Well, maybe, hang on a minute," I said as if something like not breathing can ever be a maybe. She ignored me, barreling through with a mother's calm authority. A woman doesn't carry a child through nine backbreaking months just to watch him die within twenty minutes of being home.

Holding his clenched face to my ear, I listened for the smallest hint of wind. His body flexed in the swaddle of light flannel blankets. There was nothing. It was as if there was a clamp around his throat — something blocking his airway, even though it was impossible that anything could have gotten into his mouth. It's not as if a three-day-old can wander around the corner to snack on coins and buttons. Susan was in the other room on the phone with a 911 operator. She didn't need a full assessment. He was in trouble. I called out, telling her but really telling myself not to panic, that this could be nothing, that he might be okay. As if not breathing was somehow negotiable. As if we weren't currently experiencing the clichéd nightmare of every overly nervous new parent — like a new home struck by lightning and burning to the ground, not breathing seemed an unimaginative bad joke, almost caricature.

It may have been thirty seconds. Possibly thirty-five. Susan was off the phone and standing with me. We were both on the brink of full-out panic. Our new son was tiring. His head bent forward and back, his arms waved and curled, his fists opened and closed, his shoulders rolled, his legs pedaled, but the movements were losing their gusto. He was losing the struggle. I had a thought to rifle through the kitchen drawers and get my hands on our sharpest paring knife for an attempt at a rough emergency surgery. He'd wear a jagged medallion above his collarbone — a memento of his first prank — for the rest of his life. I could have done that sooner than idly watch him fade away.

In what looked like a possible last effort to inhale, his throat produced a crisp squeak, and then another. The progress enlivened his oxygen-dry lungs, and after a few more seconds of silent exertion he managed a muted cough. His throat whistled for several breaths and after another cough and a chirp settled down into a rapid wheeze. When police arrived a minute later, he was breathing quietly and fast asleep on my shoulder.

The officers canceled the ambulance, as it seemed that the emergency had passed. Then we all pensively watched our sleeping baby. One of the officers commented that his lips looked a little blue. He was right about that. The other said something about not taking any chances with such a little one. We all agreed that even though he seemed perfectly fine, he should be taken back to the maternity floor to be examined by a doctor. With that, we rushed into the squad car and headed to the hospital with sirens blazing.

Susan and I didn't talk on the way there. Every several blocks, the officers in the front turned to ask if he was still okay. He was. I was swimming in a mixture of relief and outrage. Relief at the sight of every tiny exhalation and to be racing through and around traffic on our way to a hospital brimming with doctors who could make it right and send us home — outrage at a little soul with the temerity to come into our lives and stop breathing. I didn't expect much from a newborn, but breathing was one of them. I would expect my child to breathe at all times.

I'm not sure why I thought the doctors, after being told what happened, would be able to glance at our son and tell us he was fine and that we should just go home because we looked as though we'd collapse. It's ridiculous to think any doctor would say such a thing after being presented with a newborn whose thin lips and wrinkled palms were the color of eggplant. But he seemed fine except for that; there hadn't been the slightest indication of a replay. His breathing had been rhythmic and easy since the police arrived. I was shocked when the doctors politely told us that Casey would be admitted to the neonatal ICU for tests and observation. He would be there several days if there were no further incidents and lab results were good. Several days if we were lucky, and in the blink of an eye, surrounded by monitors, gazing helplessly along the bed rail at our son's frail body tangled in a sea net of wires and tubes, we were transported from our normal life into a tableau of unfortunate parents of a sick child.

Though I was only slightly aware of other parents perched at the rails of adjacent beds, I was keenly aware that in that moment, we were being admitted into a membership of some sort. Those we passed as we made our way to Casey's bed regarded us with blank, knowing faces. We would soon be one with them, submerged in their purgatory of emotion — joyless, but also ungrieving, consumed in a pensive unknowing that would hang from our faces like masks decorated with ornament aspects of hope.

There was an initial flurry of activity. The theme song of an ICU is the sound of rollers. Everything came to us on wheels. The approaching clatter from down the hall signified each new round of business — trays of needles and rubber strips, bags of every fluid a body might need, and all sizes of cotton batting, along with a new medical technician or nurse specialist or attending doctor with accompanying flock of residents. I scrambled to understand each procedure in order to grasp enough to have some hand in the decisions being made by these important strangers. Some took time to explain their role in the production. Most worked with their heads down while I peppered them with questions carefully constructed to convey an intelligent vigilance that might elicit an extra degree of attention and care as they poked at our son. I finally couldn't keep up and resigned myself to a sort of resentful skepticism, one that wasn't entirely un-called for — an unskilled resident had made four excruci-ating, unsuccessful attempts to thread an IV needle into Casey's veins before I was able to unmask her and demand the attending physician, who got it in on the first try.

Susan, still weak from giving birth, spent much of the time in the bathroom. It was my turn to labor with Casey. I'm not sure if my presence made his pain and trauma more tolerable, but it was the only thing I could do. He was alone. With no family for thousands of miles, I was alone too. We would be alone together. A comfort to each other on a walk through the fire. He'd take my voice and my touch, and I'd take the feeling that he needed me. I held his head in my palm, whispering in his ear as he screamed through every needle and probe put to him. It was nothing short of torture. His voice didn't last long, cracking and quickly giving away to a hoarse rasp. I stayed for every test and procedure, but there was one I couldn't watch.

A young doctor came by somewhere near the end of the onslaught and told me she would have to clear Casey's lungs. There was a chance, she said, that he might have as-pirated breast milk into his bronchial tubes during the episode back home. To leave it there would risk a lung in-fection.

The fact that she took time to explain the need for what she was going to do, without my even asking, was a bad sign. She warned me that most parents don't care to watch the procedure and asked me to step into the hall. I told her to forget it. She looked at me startled and I went on to say something about being his father and standing by him to the end of the earth. Parental bravado always used to drive me crazy — so predictable it can seem cheap, but there it was. I told her I would stay. She gave a quick nod as if she would do the same in my shoes, then turned to a tray behind her and produced a thin flexible tube about a foot long that was connected to a suction machine. She turned the machine on and after applying a thin coating of lubricant to the tube pushed its entire length into Casey's nose. He fought mightily. At only a few days old, he mustered the coordination to push with his hands and feet against the doctor's hands in what could only be an attempt to stop the violation.

It was more than I could take. It turns out the doctor was right — they often are. I held him tight but buried my face into the bed next to him. We were in hell, the place where people tell you to go when they ask how there could possibly be a God.

The onslaught eventually passed about as abruptly as it had come. Susan emerged from the bathroom and joined me at the bedside where, together, we sank into slow, quiet shock. She stroked a small spot on Casey's thigh, the only place not covered with apparatus of one sort or another. We gazed at the marquee of digital panels scrolling around the bed as if we expected to read something other than numbers, as if we expected the sequence of lights to somehow reveal the truth. I felt stupid asking, "Why?" like every other person at the blunt end of a disaster. I knew it was a worn-out maxim that this sort of thing only happens to other people, but it's how I felt. I callously scanned the babies in the other beds to find something about their health to be worse than our boy's, something to ensure that we didn't really belong here. That one's machines were bigger, the other one's were louder, with alert sounds more varied. Tubes pumping the goods in and out of that child were multicolored, another's were corrugated. I tried to somehow believe that the apparatus engulfing Casey was smaller and quieter than the others, that smooth tubing of one color meant your child wasn't as badly off.

I didn't need to look farther than a few beds down to find a boy who made Casey look like an Olympian. He was a little older and the only child who hadn't had a visitor since we'd arrived. There was something quite wrong with him. He moved very little. He didn't cry. But the most striking thing that set him apart from the rest in the unit was the total lack of any sign that someone was rooting for him. There were no flowers or cards or stuffed animals or get-well balloons, no special clothing from home or crayon drawings by an older sibling to encourage his progress. It was as if he belonged to no one. He was battling alone. The attention the nurses gave him was admirable but no substitute for a parent's bedside vigil. Our son, with his readouts ticking along predictably and the two of us stroking either side of him, had it made.

Susan's finger dropped to trace the dimples of his knee. I had no idea how she was holding up or what she was thinking. She was a coworker to me as much as a wife. We'd moved through the transition so invisibly, neither of us felt the change of altitude. For more than ten years before having a child, we'd been the most important people in each other's lives — needed most by one another and given the most. We'd spent our entire relationship on twenty-four-hour call to the smallest of each other's emotional fluctuations, discussed the ramifications and haggled through the slightest nuances of every latest film or call home to family. Now, in the midst of the greatest real drama ever to happen between us, we hadn't so much as exchanged a word. Susan's finger traced the change between us along the folds of our son's small knee. The long reign as the keeper of each other's world was suddenly over. Someone needed us more than we needed each other.

As the night closed in, hospital staff came and went, mostly checking monitor readings and fluid levels. Any results from tests that might reveal the devil wouldn't be ready until the next morning. Casey passed out, exhausted, and Susan followed on her reclining chair. I stood by a window watching the lights of the city slowly bring the skyline to life. Pedestrians poured through the streets, busy on their way like any other night at any other time. I watched them hurriedly moving in and out of a wing of the hospital just barely visible from the window and thought about our first time walking through the doors for the prenatal tour given to expecting parents. We'd waltzed in so secure in our health, arrogant and superior with knowledge. The pure joy of anticipating a child is a kind of blindness. We indulged in a google-eyed ignorance as much as any expecting couple, an amnesia about anything unjust or horrific about the world, one that allows you to prepare space in a crib and in a heart for the coming attraction. We skated past the sick and grieving nearly oblivious to them. For us, the hospital wasn't about suffering. The hospital was good. It was a joyful place. We had made the trip from sidewalk to the maternity ward several times as a drill, hurriedly scooting past the guards and up the elevator buoyed by the smiles and winks of many we passed who gave us the "any day now" kind of look. Sickness and grieving were distant continents with obscure customs. We were having a baby. Of course he'd be healthy. Most all of them are.

Most, but not all. The little girl in the bed across from us cried most of the night. Her mother leaned in to sing to her through the worst of it. I indulged in a semiconscious state between frantic moments when a jerk from Casey would set his monitors dancing. The sick boy was quiet throughout the night. Except for an occasional nurse, no one came to see him.

The following afternoon, despite being covered in tape and electrodes, despite a head full of paste-matted hair from two brain EEGs, despite over thirty needles, two sedations, ten x-rays, another lung clearing, and a tiny voice all but gone from screaming, no one was able to give more than an educated guess at why Casey had stopped breathing. I asked every staff person who appeared at the bedside, but they were as in the dark as I was. There was no reason for the episode. The mantra they all repeated was hardly a news flash: each hour that passed without a repeat was "encouraging." It seemed so thoroughly unjust, after all we'd been through, to be told what we already knew back in our apartment — that it was "encouraging" he was still breathing, ignorant as it was to believe there could be anything close to justice in a neonatal ICU — a place like a jar of dice and bullets for all its lack of predictability or fairness.

You watch someone push thirty needles into your four-day-old and it doesn't matter that they could be saving his life — a part of you wants to belt them. I began to feel primal. I was feeling my guts in a way I'd never felt them. I wanted to rip my boy from his bondage of tape and electrodes, race out of the hospital with nurses screaming, find the largest tree in the middle of an upstate forest to set him at the base of, rub soil on his head, and beg a healing from the Great Mother God.

The fact that our son's behavior had stumped all those who'd looked at him had qualified us to be seen by Doctor Narcopolis, one of the leading pediatric neurologists in New York. It was apparent from the moment we were scheduled to see her, that she held a kind of celebrity status. The overwhelming consensus of the doctors on morning rounds was that Narcopolis would get to the bottom of things. Nurses who stopped by uttered Narcopolis's name in hushed tones with reassuring nods. This was a doctor who, if unable to ferret the cause of Casey's breath-holding from the mountainous scrolls of data and monitor readouts, would simply hold our four-day-old firmly by the shoulders and have him tell her exactly what the hell he was thinking.

She came with an entourage. A thin woman in her early fifties, with wide dark eyes and a thick crop of walnut-brown hair pulled into a loose bun. Unlike the white rubber soles of all those around us, her shoes had dark, low heels. Her jewelry was expensive but understated. She had a Museum-of-Modern-Art-board-of-directors look. Her stethoscope hung like a Helmut Newton fashion accessory. Her designer glasses were new. She glanced at Susan and me, giving a small nod of acknowledgment, and turned directly to Casey as a younger man introduced her to us.

"This is Casey," she said, slowly lowering her face to him. And she did something no other staff person had done so far: she *looked* at him. The entourage stiffened their necks to see over her shoulder as she wrapped both hands around his head. "What are you doing here, Casey?" she asked, easing him with a potter's hands into various shapes. Her coordination inspired an instant confidence. She pulled Casey slowly up from the bed. The cords and tubing draped easily from his body. She was able to turn him back and forth without the tangle and abrupt stops that were so unavoidable to the rest of us. "What are you doing, Casey?" she asked again as if he might just tell her. I couldn't place her accent. It sounded exotic. It was gorgeous, although I'm sure that if she spoke with mud in her mouth, it would have sounded gorgeous to me — everything about her was gorgeous. The deeper she looked into our son, the more gorgeous she became. Her slow, exacting rhythm set her apart, not just from her colleagues and the hospital itself but from the entire medical establishment. The doctors on their rounds were right: this was a person who could get to the bottom of things.

"Hello, Casey . . . hello, Casey." She held him like a fine, large ruby, turning him slowly under her careful jeweler's gaze, speaking directly into his face, giving him a slight shake and then watching. There was something almost shaman-like about her. She had all the accoutrements of Western medicine hanging from her neck and out of her pockets, but they were all left idle as she used only her senses to find in this exquisite gem the flaw that might cause it to break into pieces at a touch.

"Let me check something," she said, suddenly looking at me over the top of her elegant glasses. "Here, papa." I took him gently from her hands. "Hold him close to this rail," she instructed. It was the metal railing of the headboard. She pulled a large tuning fork from her lab coat and slammed its metal handle sharply against it. Casey jumped. Narcopolis smiled. "He can hear us," she said. "Good." Surrounded by a hundred thousand dollars worth of cutting-edge technology and the leading pediatric neurologist in New York was beating the headboard with a stick. There was something reassuring about that.

Narcopolis finished her examination, running through the gamut of newborn reflexes with Casey's full cooperation. He proved himself a fully equipped model, grasping, flexing, startling, arching, stepping, and turning as designed. Each behavior was followed by a curt "Good" by Narcopolis. She put on a glove and slipped her finger into his mouth. It took a little rub of his palate to get him to suck. "A little weak," she said. He hadn't been breastfed since being admitted. A little reluctance on that front seemed appropriate. She laid him gently back in his bed and finished by cooing an apology into his ear. He slept instantly.

After scratching some notes to herself, she gave Casey a long look and then gazed at the monitors chirping monotonously at our shoulders before turning back to me.

"This is what I think, papa," she began. "The episode will not be repeated. Casey will not stop breathing again. He's a good boy. All of the tests show results within normal healthy ranges. There is a slightly elevated thickness along a particular region of his brain — show them the film." A woman in the group produced an x-ray of Casey's head, which she held up to a window. Narcopolis indicated the offending area. "Still within normal limits," she continued. "Nothing to be concerned about, but coupled with the episode, it makes me think a little bit. Although I believe Casey is out of danger, I am not altogether comfortable with his situation until I know what exactly produced the crisis."

Susan exhaled. She knew what was coming. "I want to watch him another night. We need to do another EEG as well." Narcopolis read the fatigue written across our faces — familiar lines for a doctor who has spent a career watching parents of sick children try to dig their way out of a collapsing pit of sand.

"He slept through the last EEG?" she asked.

"No," I said. "He had to be sedated."

"Maybe he sleeps for this one," she said, looking down at him, stroking his head. "And you just washed the paste from his hair." Susan smiled through tears and nodded. "The paste doesn't bother him," Narcopolis went on. "I know you want to bring him out of this place, but we shouldn't take a chance with such a little one. I'll order the EEG for this afternoon," she said, gathering her things to leave. "When he's done, mama, you can begin breastfeeding."

That evening we endured a final visit from the same resident who had done such a poor job of starting Casey's IV. She had come to us several times during our stay to work on him. Most of what she did seemed meaningless and caused discomfort. During this last encounter, she spent several minutes in front of her fellow residents, twisting Casey's legs into his chest and making him scream — "checking his hips," she instructed her colleagues. I asked if she wouldn't mind doing her demonstration on a newborn who felt a little more mended, one with parents who were a little fresher. I assured her his hips had been examined by his pediatrician the day he was born and asked what hips had to do with breathing in the first place. She didn't have a good answer but took the opportunity to demonstrate the good doctor by hailing me with her most understanding expressions and empathetic phrases. My throat shook as I asked her to leave us. She gave Casey another twist to make it seem to the group as though she was finishing up and then bade farewell. I nodded civilly but felt more like jumping her shoulders and ripping her hair out with my teeth. I'd had enough. I might have felt differently if Casey seemed sick, but he didn't seem sick. He seemed exhausted, agitated, depleted, violated, but not sick. For committing the minor infraction of clenching his throat a few seconds, he'd been dredged through hell. The punishment no longer fit the crime.

After a couple of attempts, Susan had some minor success with breastfeeding. I tried to blot out the sounds of monitors and crying babies as I watched the two of them, imagining we were in our bedroom with the lights turned low. Despite the setting, the feeding made us all feel better. The floor began to quiet down as the night pulled in.

By eight o'clock, it was mostly parents at the bedsides. Except, of course, for the sick boy who was still alone. The unit wasn't filled to capacity, so the staff had made an effort to space us all as far apart as possible. Because of that, except for an occasional flurry I had been barely aware of the life-and-death dramas playing out around us. As with our child, many of the other children were all but obscured by machinery. You couldn't get a look at them without being deliberate about it. But with no parents or relatives around his bed, the sick boy was fair game for long, curious stares. You could walk right up to him. There was no invisible privacy barrier to break through, no feeling that you were stepping behind the counter. The boy was public property. Because he belonged to no one, he belonged to everyone.

Susan and Casey were sleeping comfortably by ten o'clock, so I decided to step out of the hospital for my first breath of fresh air in two days. I got a tuna fish sandwich with a ginger ale and ate it standing under a street lamp. Twenty minutes later, I returned to the unit to find a stocky Hispanic man and little girl standing at the sick boy's bedside. Next to them, a woman sat on a chair against the wall. The little girl held the boy's hand. The man stroked his head.

"I think it's his family," Susan whispered as I sat down.

"Have they said anything?"

"Mostly Spanish."

The man looked over to us briefly. Susan and I nodded hello and he nodded back. The woman looked over and smiled. I waved. There wasn't more than fifteen feet between us, but the invisible barriers encapsulating each family in the unit made it seem as though we were exchanging glances from passing vehicles. The girl looked over to us and something in her expression reached just over the barrier. I went to say hello.

"Hey, I was wondering who this guy belonged to," I said as I approached. "He's your brother?" She looked into his face and nodded.

"How you doing?" the man asked.

"Hanging in there," I said. "I guess we could all be better, huh?" The woman smiled quickly.

"My wife doesn't speak English," the man said with a thick accent. "She was in a coma after the baby come out. Four days. The doctors say she almost didn't make it. But she did — thank God. I almost lost her and the baby. I almost lost both of them."

The near-miss experience that lands you in an intensive care unit has a way of stripping you of any pretext. The man's sudden openness didn't catch me off guard as it would have a few days ago. Forty-eight nervewracking hours of listening to the chirps and squeaks of my son's vital signs had brought me to the understanding that parents of sick children aren't a membership as much as a race, and with race comes brotherhood and with brotherhood, openness. Both of us wore the evidence of our all-night vigils in unshaven faces and wrinkled, slept-in clothing. I could somehow tell he hadn't talked with another man since his ordeal began and wondered if he could sense it was the same with me. Suddenly, there was nothing I wouldn't reveal to this complete stranger.

"We was at a party," he continued. "Everybody just eating and dancing and we was just laughing with everybody. Then my wife, she start to feel the baby coming. We was driving to the hospital and the baby, he start to come out too fast right there in the seat. Then my wife pass out with a seizure and the baby coming out. I pull the car over and try to get some help from somebody. Then I try to helping her. The ambulance came, but then the baby, he stop coming out. It's no good, the guys they say — it's no good the baby stop coming now. So they taking her to the hospital to get the baby out but my wife, the doctor say he don't know if she gonna make it. They took the baby out, but he didn't get enough oxygen and my wife was in a coma for four days. Can you believe that? Then I was too busy — first I'm with her to make sure she makes it, then I'm have to take care of my daughter. It's too many things — I hardly get to see the baby."

The girl said something to her dad in Spanish and he nodded. She went over to a lung-clearing device like the one used on Casey. A long tube connected to a machine on a chrome stand. Nothing more than a glorified shop vac as far as I could tell, wrapped on three sides with a vast array of lights and meters. The girl turned it on and used the tube to slowly clear her brother's mouth. She couldn't have been more than eight years old. She moved with a precision and care that other girls her age use to set up a tea party or straighten a doll's hair.

"I thank God they made it," the man said almost to himself.

"He's gonna be okay?" I asked.

"The doctors say he didn't get enough oxygen, so maybe he's gonna have some kind of problems. That's why my daughter and me, we gonna learn to take care of him. He don't cough. We gotta keep him clean with the machine until he learns how." The little girl finished her brother with a wipe of his chin and replaced the tube in its holder. "She's already getting good at it — look at that." the man said proudly. "Just like the nurse."

"Only better," I said. "Because she loves him." The man didn't hear me. "She's a good sister," I continued, my voice tripping. The girl looked at me. "You're taking care of your little brother, huh?" She nodded. "He's a lucky little boy to have a sister like you."

The girl took a brush from a metal drawer and began to lovingly draw its soft bristles through the boy's hair. I was caught completely off guard by a wash of emotion. I had only walked over to say a simple hello and good luck, and suddenly I felt an enormous kinship with a man whose name I hadn't yet learned. We silently watched his daughter brush her brother's head, long after the fine hairs were put in their place. The man who'd watched his wife have a baby and a seizure at the same time in the backseat of a car, whose new son didn't cough, looked at his family with a joy that lit up walls.

By the time he looked over at me, I had given in to tears. His face widened into a smile and tears dropped from his eyes as well. Like me, he fought them at first. We sort of shook our heads and tried to laugh around them, but they came down harder. So we both stood there, crying for no reason we could have actually stated. Though I'd had plenty of reason to, I hadn't cried once since Casey's "episode," as we now called it. The man reached out and touched my shoulder as if to tell me it would be okay, we would make it somehow because we were all alive and that's all that mattered. His wife and son all but consumed by the sandy pit and he was comforting me.

"How's your baby?" he asked, his voice cracking.

"I think he's gonna be okay," I said, wiping my arm across my eyes. "He's fine, actually. He stopped breathing back at home. It was stupid. He's okay now."

"Then you gonna leave here," he said, smiling. "That's good."

I walked over to the girl and leaned down to look at her baby brother a last time. "He's gonna be a good little brother," I said.

"He *is* a good little brother," she returned.

"What's his name?"

"Salvio."

"Salvio," I repeated. "Brave little Salvio."

The man beamed at the foot of the bed. "In Spanish, it means 'Gift from God.'"

Next morning's visit by Narcopolis brought no new information. She asked us to stay another night but said we could go home if we made an appointment with her the next day. We chose to leave.

I drove our truck from the parking lot to the front doors of the hospital as I had several days earlier, to bring Casey home once again. The first time was a rehearsal. This was the second chance most parents don't get. This time I wasn't thinking about phone calls I had to make or work I had to catch up on. I didn't argue with Susan about how to secure the belt around the car seat or keep the blanket out of Casey's face. There was no camera for pictures, no perfect little outfit to mark the arrival with booties that didn't stay on and knitted caps that looked better in gift wrapping than on a baby's head. All that mattered was that we were going home.

On the drive back, I couldn't help but notice the difference between going home with a new baby and going home with a new baby after grappling with the real possibility that we might not have been able to. The two experiences were so close together that in the silence between us, as we drove away from the hospital, it was hard to miss a joy that was deeper this time around. Gratitude in the wind of a passing bullet. I was certain I felt better than any other new father who might be bringing his child home for the first time on that day — better than any of them but not as good as the man in the hospital who'd one day take home his little Salvio.

Although the cause of Casey's breath-holding was never discovered, to this day the episode hasn't been repeated. Casey breathes like any other kid.

Very encouraging.

THE SPECIAL TREAT

I often spend the first few hours of the day behind the barn splitting wood. There's nothing that I know of that makes you feel your body in quite the same way as burning through twenty or so logs with a maul on a cold morning. It's impossible to harbor any feeling of insignificance as you're busting the monsters apart. Heats you twice, the old-timers say. Near-zero weather in a T-shirt is just fine once you get going.

The maul I use is a twenty-pound iron wedge welded to a thirty-inch pipe. It's red. An easy hit sends a medium-sized log flying apart. A well-placed, full-powered hit goes through a log two feet wide. Most of the beasts I'm pounding are at least that big.

The logs are from two trees that fell on the house within the first weeks of our moving in. The first one ripped out the electricity and telephone. The second fell mainly on the garage. Catalpa trees. Giants of the forest. I measured the trunks and came up with sixteen feet around for one and twelve for the other — a magnitude that on any other tree would be a sign of stoic perseverance. In a catalpa, it's a sign of gluttony. The catalpa puts its weight on quickly. Trees that look hundreds of years old are usually closer to thirty. The result is a massive structure that's short on engineering. Like a house plant gone wild. A big show with very little planning. The whole truth is that the catalpa is nothing more than a giant mushroom disguised as a tree.

Neither one fell in a storm; they both succumbed to their own voracious growth, giving way under the sheer weight of their enormous limbs. I had the first one cut up and hauled behind the barn. When the second one went down a week later, I bought a chain saw, figured out how to use it, cut it up and hauled it back myself.

Now they're a mass of logs.

The boys sit on a nearby pile of them, bundled so tight they move like stiff old men. They watch quietly as I swing through a few dozen before laying the maul on the ground to wait out a small sprain in my wrist. It pulls through like a needle and thread as I roll my hand in a slow circle. The pain is minor, but the weight of the maul demands a full-power grip. For now, I have to stop.

I look to the boys, who are motionless in their layers of clothing — hoods pulled snug around the kind of red-cheeked, flat expressions that only the cold air can produce. Casey is three and four months. We just celebrated the fact yesterday. At this age, you celebrate the months. Owen is a stumbling drunk one-year-old. They're both warmly wrapped but that's all I'll take credit for. There's absolutely no coordination to their gear. We have a basket of hand-me-down scarves, mittens, hats, and boots that have been once worn by no less than six different families. Matching outfits can be constructed with effort, but on most mornings, I reach into the middle of the pile and pull out whatever fits around whatever limb I'm holding. They each have a warm outfit that would put them within a fair shot of the busiest baby model, but those kinds of clothes wear better on a walk through a studio two-shot than over a burly pile of catalpa.

Behind us, the woods are alive with gusts of wind. Wood chips under my feet and the sound of the stream crashing through the rocks, the bright cool sun and the possibility of a bear-sighting at any moment — I'll never know where I'd be standing on this day had Casey not decided to close up his throat as a two-day-old. I don't think it would be here. The thrill of his arrival followed so closely by the threat of his departure sharpened Susan and me somehow. Without ever discussing it outright, we both knew that child care was out of the question. In the month of follow-up clinic visits, Dr. Narcopolis and the most sophisticated diagnostics in pediatric neurology had assured us that Casey would *probably* be fine. No one could guarantee it wouldn't happen again. It was enough to make us aware, on a certain level, of his every breath. We were counting.

In the city, Susan and I engaged in the frantic juggle of work and baby care most new parents go through. With no family in the area, we juggled alone — schedules, bottles, appointments, diapers, phone calls — hundreds and hundreds of phone calls that seemed so important at the time and so impossible to complete without interruptions. I was just so-so at it. Susan was much better at keeping the balls in the air. Her pattern was tight; most of the time she whirled them around her head and behind her back with effortless grace. I was adept at tossing and catching a single ball but could never graduate to actual juggling. At my best, I could go a few moments before everything crashed down around me — baby Casey screaming and me late for work. We cobbled out a fair existence, but it wasn't what you'd call a home life.

So I'm not sure what we were thinking when we decided to have Owen; logic rarely comes into this kind of decision. It was like, I haven't slept for over a year, my back is killing me, my hair is falling out, but I love what this kid is doing to me — let's have another one.

Unlike his older brother, who had been long in the making, Owen was eager for this world. Susan became pregnant at the thought of him. We would do it all again, but something was immediately different this time around. More than Casey, Owen had the power to force us to become a family, to find this farmhouse in Cherry Valley. He would have been happy enough to sleep in a box or a drawer, happy enough with the small patch of grass growing from the window box, but we went out and bought these twelve and a half acres, a barn, several outbuildings, and a two-story house. Owen forced us to go beyond simple functioning, beyond providing for each other: he had compelled us to make a life. When Casey was born, he got a quilt and a rocking chair. Owen got the farm.

"Come over here, guys," I say. "I've got a special treat."

The words "special treat" have always held a kind of spell over them. At the mere mention, they drop anything, no matter how good, to come investigate. They'd walk through a fire with smiles on for a special treat. I've never abused the power of those words, always delivering on their promise.

The boys climb cautiously down the jagged wood pile and stand at my feet. I raise an eyebrow and ask them if they're ready — presentation is always a big part of a special treat. Casey nods eagerly. Owen's eyes are wide and waiting.

"What is it?" Casey asks. Could be anything from Popsicle to bug, and special, by God. He knows it. Always special.

"Behind my back," I say. His face goes from curious to puzzled as I present a small, fresh split of wood from the center of an enormous log. "Does this look special?" I ask.

"Maybe," Casey says, as if hoping for some rainbow of candy to spring out. Owen's eyes are lit. For him, a special treat is all presentation. He's satisfied with the wood as is.

"Here. Hold it," I say. They grasp either end. Casey's eyes are the very color of anticipation. Owen begins a tug-of-war but stops when I put my hand on his back. "Does it feel special?" I ask.

"I don't know," Casey returns, his voice brimming with possibility. Owen tugs.

"Smell it," I say. "Put your nose right on it."

Casey does. Owen follows. And just above the wood, their eyes flatten into smiles. I crouch down and press my nose to the other side of the piece, and the three of us hold fast, our faces to the wood. Horizontal rays of morning sun shoot through the forest and play against the tall silver planks of the barn. A breeze sets the shadows in motion. I'm facing the boys eyeball to eyeball as we breathe the aroma. Owen is snorting. Casey waves his mittens through the steam rising from my shoulders. These are the good old days. They feel so short, even as we live them, as if they've already happened — these years when the thrills come straight out of the ground. The world owns them by five — at three and a half and almost two, Casey and Owen are still their own. They're still wild.

Owen tugs and gets it this time, walking away with the wood to his face. Casey wants his own piece, so I split one off and he sits down with it pressed to his nose. He tells me it smells good. Wants to know why. I tell him what I know about the middle of a tree, which is not that much but enough for this moment — that it's been long in the making and hasn't yet been touched, so it's still pure, still tender, in a way that's revealed only in its beautiful smell. Owen stands at the edge of the forest with his head down against his small piece. He's still snorting.

My wrist throbs lightly. I try a few more hits, but it's no good. I slip on my jacket, brush wood chips from my hair, and call the boys down to the house for hot chocolate in sippy cups on the porch.

There's a tarp-covered, hydraulic splitter in every other backyard in the valley. There was a time when I would have borrowed one and taken care of this mountain of logs in a single afternoon. I was more efficient before having children. Now, because of them, it's different. It has to be. With this and with everything, there's more in the process than there is in the finished job. I find myself looking for the path more than for the destination.

All children, as they look to define who they are, ask their parents to reveal themselves — reveal what they stand for, what they stand against, what they live for, what they would die for. In every moment of every day, Casey and Owen beg me to show them who I am, so I concentrate on the path. The path reveals you in a way the destination never could. I used to fight the process. Now I see where it takes me. Most times, with their hands in the middle of everything, there's hardly a choice. After a whole morning of splitting wood, firewood is the smallest piece of what I end up with. The process has become the end in itself. The process has become the destination.

So I'll turn these logs into pieces that will dry and burn by next season, but I'll sprain my wrist again.

Produce another special treat.

Stop to smell the inside of a tree.

And if I'm lucky, the fireplace will roar with heat and my boys will cherish, as I have, the memory of a father who splits wood.

THE OLD MAN

PART TWO

I f we're not in the woods, we're on the road.

Nothing beats a backpack and stroller ride down the valley. Owen could not be happier with the sprig of flowering
chicory he holds high and waves through the clouds. Casey's
stooped over the front rail, thrilled with his grapevine click-
clacking against the stroller's spokes.

We approach the house where the old man works, and
from the road I can see his blue Pontiac spread like a welcome mat across the blacktop. His head is in the trunk. We
turn off the road and walk down the long drive to say hello.
He's still in the trunk when we reach him but pops up teeth
first when Casey says hello. He's in a white shirt and
painter's pants with a horsehair brush in a worn leather holster slung low around his hips. His red face is freckled with
white paint.

"Well, how are my two deputies this morning?" he says with a welcoming laugh. "Good to see ya, Marc."

"Thought we'd stop by on our walk," I say.

"Why, sure. I was hoping you guys would come by one of these days."

"Saw your car from the road."

"You know," he says suddenly serious, "I got this car for practically nothing, and it runs like a top. I haven't done a thing to it. Boy, and the trunk holds just about anything. Sure."

Casey holds out his grapevine for Dick, who crouches down and looks it over as if it's the first one he's ever seen.

"You put it in the spokes when your Dad pushes the stroller?" he asks. Casey grins and nods. "Oh boy, that makes a good racket, doesn't it? Why, sure it does — oh, you bet."

I let Owen out of the backpack and he walks directly over to Dick, reaching to his hip to run his fingers through the soft black hairs of the paintbrush.

"Well, look at this one," Dick says as he pulls the brush out like an old Colt from its holster and lowers it to Owen. It's a gorgeous, well-used old thing — a pecan-colored beaver-tail handle with a wide oval heel and battered leather-bound ferrule. Owen smiles at him while twirling his hands through the bristle. "I should of brought my camera," Dick says. "Oh boy." Casey drops his vine and runs over to join Owen. The two of them race their fingers through the brush. Dick tosses his head back in a long laugh.

"Okay, guys," I say. "C'mon, stop bothering him."

"Oh, it's okay, dad," Dick returns. "These little guys couldn't bother me if they tried."

It was true. I don't know why I tried to stop them. They couldn't bother him any more than he could bother them. Old men and little boys are on the same side of the coin somehow. It's thirty-five-year-olds who can be the bother.

"You boys like that brush, don't you?" he says with another long laugh. "I like it too. I run my fingers through it just like that sometimes. You bet. Oh, it's fun to play with." Then he looks at me. "They don't make them like this anymore," he says. "Boy, and if you find one in a store, they're asking a fortune for it. Sure."

A little later, the boys start to get fussy. I tell Dick I have to go. "Oh, they're all right," he says. "What's the hurry? Here, I got something to fix them." Soon, the three of them are sitting on the huge blue seat of the Pontiac. Dick has opened a bag of peanut chews that he pulled from the glove compartment, and the three of them dig in. Casey holds a melted fistful in each hand. A thin chocolate river flows from Owen's mouth into his shirt. Needless to say, they're all smiles — the fussing has stopped. "I know just how they feel," Dick says, with chocolate sitting in the corners of his mouth. "It's why I keep these here in the Pontiac with me."

When I was a little older than Casey, I used to sit with my grandmother at the dining room table, chewing through handfuls of hard candy. She'd eat almost as many as I would while poring over a crossword. The two of us could go through a whole bag. I don't recall my parents or any of my aunts or uncles ever stopping to have one. It struck me as strange even at that young age that if they were so good, why did no one but Grandma and I eat them?

Dick offers me the bag of chews, but I decline. He asks if I'm sure. He says they're good — that he's gotta watch it because he could eat a whole bag of them. I imagine that if I wasn't there, it's just what would happen. He says I should take one for later. I tell him I'm okay. I don't care for peanut chews. He shrugs as Owen reaches for another. I think about how they're ruining their appetite for lunch, about how they're ruining their teeth, about how they'll need showers when they're done. I'm about to say something when I can almost hear the old man's voice cutting me off. *Oh, hey, they're such good fellas, what's the harm?*

I decide to keep my mouth shut. I'll hose them off and brush their teeth soon enough. What's the harm? I'll make them eat peas at supper. They'll survive. Sometimes you have to watch it when you're a grown-up. It's hard not to be a bother.

When we finally turn to leave, Owen falls and hits his lip on the blacktop. He looks up from the driveway and unleashes an accusatory wail. A red pearl of blood sprouts up like a reprimand — I should have stopped him from running, I should have been there to catch him. But it's only a bump. I race to pick him up, feeling like an amateur. He doesn't want to be coddled. He straight-arms my attempts to console him. Needs to scream a little. I figure it out only after several rebukes. The old man has disappeared. I turn around and find him once again with his head in the trunk.

For Dick, the Pontiac is more than just a vehicle — it's a handbag. He emerges with a piece of gauze and an antiseptic swab.

"He's all right," he says, handing me the gauze. I press it to Owen's lip and the bleeding stops. Dick hands me the swab. "I thought I was the only one around here who'd need these," he says. "Always tripping over or bumping into something around here. It's why I keep them in the Pontiac. Sure. It's good to have 'em handy." I pass the swab over Owen's lip, and he's all better. He hops from my knee and runs off. "Look at him go," Dick says. "Oh boy. Us big guys fall harder."

"You have grandchildren, Dick?"

"I have a granddaughter and a grandson," he says with a proud look that's an obvious feed for the next question.

"Got pictures?" I ask.

"Why, sure, you bet," he says pulling out a wallet and opening it to a portrait studio shot of a boy just younger than Owen. "That's the grandson. It's my son's boy. Oh and he's a good one — already sleeps through the night. Can you believe it?"

"Don't even tell me that," I say. "Casey's still getting up — we did it all wrong."

"And here's my granddaughter," he says. I look at her but can't help noticing the facing picture of a young woman.

"And who is this young lady?" I ask. Dick's face goes dim. The light pulls right out of it.

"That's my daughter that died, Marc."

"I don't think I knew about that," I say after a moment. I

look at the girl, frozen in time, and then at the granddaughter, his grief and gladness facing each other and then pressed together as he closes the billfold. From land mines to confetti, anything can happen on a glance through an old man's wallet. I feel like I've accidentally stepped into a secret room that I'm not sure how to exit.

"Died in childbirth," he says. "The baby too. They both died."

"How long ago?"

"Few years back."

"That's uh . . . how? . . . how could that — I didn't think that happened anymore."

"The doctors don't know why. They say they just lost her. Then they tried to save the baby. I guess it happens sometimes." The boys are in a field, chasing each other in circles. In a moment, the world seems as terrifying as it is beautiful.

"That's something you never get over," he says with a sudden look of clarity.

"I can't imagine." The boys collapse and lie against each other in the tall grass.

"No," he says, "you can't."

We walk out to the field where they're lying. Owen has his feet against Casey's ribs. He gives a push and they both laugh. Dick helps me load them into the stroller and backpack. "I gotta see if I can get some lunch into these guys," I say.

"Oh boy," Dick says with a smile. "Good luck. I don't think we'll be hungry until dinner — that bag of chews is almost empty."

Visiting with Dick has become a required part of our walks through the valley. If I pass the house without stopping, the boys both throw up a protest. I tell myself their affection is only about peanut chews and the paintbrush in the trunk but have to secretly admit that there's more to it than that. They yell when I pass the driveway because they want to see the old man who trips on his feet and gets fussy between sweets. They yell because they want to visit with one of their own.

GOD AND ANGELS

Despite the fact that we've lived here over a year now, I'm still not clear on the best way to get through a cold, rainy day without the three of us clawing the walls. The boys sense the chilly dampness in the air even before they open their eyes. They both wake up crying. Susan has already left for work. She does her best to set us up before leaving, but some mornings it's just no use.

I'm at my worst in the first half hour of the day. Many times, the boys aren't much better. Along with blow-drying her hair, lacing her boots, and gathering her supplies for a full day of teaching, Susan will usually try to give me a jump on the day by cutting up some fruit and filling the sippy cups. While I sit at the kitchen table staring at a coffee, she's putting stamps on the bills that can go out, making a list of needed groceries, loading the washing machine, laying out shoes and hats and gloves, and doing it all with lipstick in one hand and mascara in the other. Every morning, she's a hero.

I know there are times when she wonders why I don't just jump up and get the day going the way she would, with the crayons in a line and paintbrushes ready to go. But one of the best things about Susan is that she lets me be the other parent. She doesn't expect me to play an equal role in raising the boys only to go crazy when I don't do things exactly as she would. She never makes me feel like the sitter, or that she's better at all this, even when she is. Susan respects my rhythm as a father and lets me find my way for better and for worse.

This morning, it's for worse.

I make oatmeal that neither of them eats. Too hot and then too cold. Toys go flying across the room because they want *that* one, no — *that* one, no — the *other* one. The TV is too loud and then too soft and on the wrong channel as well. They're both too cold. The blanket is "too picky" and too big for one but too small to share. They want the same cup and the same banana and the same book at the same time. Shampoo bottles in the toilet and then they're both wailing — Owen wants a knife and Casey wants a wine-glass. A half hour feels like three weeks, and I don't need a house with windows to know it's raining out.

Fighting this sort of thing could end in disaster, so I take the only reasonable action and haul us outside for a walk between the clouds before someone loses an eye.

The road is a black mark drawn into the thickest smoke. Because the valley is high, there are spots between fog banks that are crystal clear — we are literally walking through the clouds. I don a hunter's-orange baseball cap to distract commuters from their books-on-tape just long enough to veer around us as they roll by. The stroller is big enough to hold both boys with blankets and toys; its cavernous metal frame draped with wet cloth jumps and sways with the ruts in the road. I'm pushing a gypsy's wagon with two foul little trolls on a trip through the soup.

People who pass think I'm crazy. I'm sure of it. In the comfort of their leather-appointed, leased vehicles, half-listening to the latest Mary Higgins Clark or Danielle Steel, a Danish in the passenger seat, a coffee in the holder, they pass us and feel sorry for the boys whose father takes them along a cold, rain-soaked street at seven in the morning. If the sight of us fails to inspire pity, it most certainly sparks suspicion. Fathers don't push strollers along this road. Even in the midday sun. And it's the crack of dawn. And the wind is howling. I'm in knee-high English Wellies and a barn jacket over a down coat. The boys are in blankets. Don't forget the hat. We look insane.

A mile from the house. The commuters are gone, the road is ours. It's quiet except for the skidding sound of my boots and an occasional roll of thunder. Thick bands of fog coil through the forest, following us along the road like giant gray boas. Trees along the highest ridges of either side of the valley are so dark with rain they look purple. The air about them is steeped with hidden meanings and things not quite understandable.

Owen begins a song, the kind we all must have sung at one and a half — the perfect song, his tongue clicking and rolling through random notes. The sound of water over rocks. Doves. Wind. I'm consumed by its smallness. My throat is quiet but my blood is singing. In his soft perfection, I'm suddenly aware of my own most perfect side. It's him. I've always known that treating your child badly is nothing more than the deepest form of self-loathing, but I never considered that it could go the other way; that one of the most stirring things a child offers you is the opportunity to know the most perfect version of yourself. Once you find that out — from the moment you've caught a glimpse of it — there's only one way to love them, and it has more to do with the way you feel about yourself than with anything else. Without words, Owen's song gives the most convincing evidence I have ever heard that I should fall utterly in love with myself.

The music continues as a silhouette slowly emerges in the distance. Casey sees before I do. Tells me it's a man, and he's right. Walking toward us, short and round, his legs ticking rhythmically beneath him. Owen brings his song to a close and straightens his back to get a better look. As we approach each other, the man's face pinches into a wide, flat smile. He's in his fifties, short and stout—the figure of a teapot.

"Well, I'd ask what the heck you're doing out in this weather, but then I'd have to answer it for myself first," he says. He looks down to the boys, giving them a warm hello, and is very gracious as they stare blankly back at him.

"Not too friendly this morning," I say. He asks if I'm new to the area. I tell him I am and wonder what tipped him off. The blaze orange hat makes for a pretty authentic local look. The Wellies might have given me away. I claim my Wisconsin roots but tell him we've moved here from New York.

"I used to live in New York City myself," he says. "How about that."

"We're everywhere," I say, ominously. He laughs.

"We spread and multiply," he returns, his cheeks bulging, the skin smooth and red under his eyes practically lighting up the road.

"What did you do in New York?"

"Florist," he says with the slightest puff in his chest. "I had a shop. Then I moved out here and opened one. My son runs it now — he's a florist. We're both florists. I'm retired, but I stop in a couple days a week to make him crazy when he gets behind. He needs me. Some of the weddings out here — major Rodgers and Hammerstein productions."

"Some of the houses out here — I'm not surprised."

"And the funerals? Some of them" — his arms fly out like a bad actor's — "they spend their whole life in the Poconos, and when they die they want Hawaii." He waits for the laugh and I insert one in the right place. "And my son can do it — turn an Elk's Lodge into a luau if they say so. He's good."

Thunder sounds in the distance and rolls invisibly along the rim of the horizon. Against the foreboding landscape, the man's cheer is almost jarring. There's something about him that doesn't fit — a contradiction, something in his eyes that betrays him. The boys are silent. I know without even looking at them that they are mesmerized, as I am, by this round, retired florist. He's something of a spectacle. We watch him as we would a Roman candle or midnight bonfire, gratefully riding the rhythms of this new face. The man has given us a reason to be on the road. He's become the destination, what we've been looking for to take us away from each other.

"Works out good for me," he continues. "I make a few arrangements, do some orders, help with the books. Once a florist . . ."

"Is that true?" I ask. I've handed him the wheel. The boys not screaming and I want him to tell me everything about being a florist. Baby's breath. Bitterroot wreaths. Boutonnieres. Bleeding hearts.

"Some guys retire and all they want to do is play around. I like working too much. On the other hand, making a corsage isn't laying bricks, I guess."

"That's true."

"What do you do?"

"Well, . . . mostly, I try to keep these boys from tearing the walls down."

"You take care of your boys?"

"Yeah, on good days anyway. We take care of each other, really. I just change the diapers."

Thunder sounds again, closer this time. The highest branches begin to hiss with wind. Field sparrows dart low along the ground, vanishing and reappearing with each stop and start. A fat drop of rain hits the road like an egg.

"You believe in angels?" the man asks suddenly, his shiny black eyes pouring heat.

"Gosh . . . ," I say, startled by the question. "I'm not sure. I don't know."

"Oh, they exist," he says. "They exist."

"You think?" I ask, a little disappointed and bracing for what might be next.

"Oh, I know they do. I've seen them," he says, his cheeks burning bright red, his head nodding slowly. And suddenly, I feel as though I have to head back home. A dark army of approaching clouds, scraping gasps of wind, scowling commuters, even the random splatter of swollen raindrops haven't convinced me to turn around, but the possibility of a back-and-forth through the "Are you saved?" labyrinth does. I feel let down; his outward appearance held so much more promise than this. But the commuters were right, only a crazy person would be on the road right now. One talking angels. The other in an orange hat with the babies in a cart. A hell of a storm about to tip over, and they aren't even moving. Totally crazy or just very dumb and probably both.

"You can live your whole life without knowing they're all around you," the man says, still nodding. I pull the flaps of my hat down over my ears and batten down the boys' hatches. "But I can't tell you how good it feels to find out sooner. To find out they're here with us — here with you and me and those boys right now. I wish someone would've told me earlier, when I was a young man like you, even though I probably wouldn't have believed in them until I saw one. Still, I wish someone would have tried to tell me. A lot of people know as sure as a hand raised up to the sky — they're with us."

". . . Well, it looks like that rain's coming."

"The fact is, I shouldn't be standing here in front of you talking like this right now. I should be buried in the mud with my wife and sons up by the little church up here." He pauses. "My house caught on fire."

And that stops me. Because he means it. He should be dead. His wife and sons should be dead. It's hard not to be stopped by a person who says a thing like that and means it.

"The middle of the night," he continues. "My whole family inside. Sleeping. Bedrooms on the top — all these old houses, bedrooms on the top. Staircase becomes a chimney and you're dead before you even see it coming. I shouldn't be standing here. They exist. That's a fact. I'm the proof."

"How did it happen?"

"I don't really know what happened — how it happened. All I can tell you is that I was woken in the middle of the night to my name being called out, and I open my eyes and there's this large, glowing figure at my bedroom door — this beautiful being like I'd never even seen in a dream. It told me there was a fire, that it hadn't reached us yet, it was downstairs, but that it would choke us out in less than a minute. Then it came to me right as I laid there — just *leaned* into me, filled me up in a way. *Wake your wife,* it said. *Get your sons* — HURRY. I sat up, shaking my head. The first wisps of smoke started billowing in."

He's gazing past me now, the horror of the night reflecting in his eyes more vividly than anything he could reveal with words. This is his story. The one he has to tell — *my house burned down, I was saved by an angel* — the thing that cracked a hole in him and all he can do is let it pour out around the feet of anyone who doesn't walk away first. What I say or do is unimportant. This isn't a conversation. This is him. This is his story. It's all he has — all anyone has: their story. And it's an amazing thing when a complete stranger walks up and hands theirs to you.

"You see, and that's the funny part," he says, his eyes resting just above my shoulder, "I was woken up before the smoke. That's the part that always keeps me clear about what happened when I think back on it — why I can never deny the main point about all this — that the whole thing started with an angel. Because I sleep like a rock through anything. But I woke up that night. And I knew about the fire before the smoke. And that is something."

He leans down to look at Owen and reaches out to touch his head, his sleeve pulling back to reveal an armful of fire's paisley scars.

"Little one's asleep on his chin," he says and then looks to Casey. "Not here."

"Casey never sleeps," I say, only half-joking. The man ignores me. He and Casey are staring at each other.

"You've got an angel, Casey," he says warmly. "Whether or not you or your little brother or dad ever believe it. There's one with each of you."

He rises from his crouch and looks into my eyes with a smile and a wink. "I think you're right about that rain," he says. "You better get on home and get those boys inside. It's gonna be a good one. We'll see you around." He turns to leave, looking over his shoulder to offer one last bit of advice. "Oh — and you know, around here it's just a matter of time."

"Yeah," I said. "What?"

"You hit a deer." He throws his arms out in a what-are-you-gonna-do gesture. "Just hope it's not a buck."

Halfway back to the house and the wind has gone from intermittent suggestion to full argument. The tar is spotted with rain at some spots and dry bones at others. Behind us the sky growls like a dog on a chain. Owen is out cold. His head rests against the front rail of the stroller. Casey is lost in a world of his own. He surfaces every now and again to ask if I'm pushing them fast. Yes, I tell him. Why am I pushing them fast, he wants to know. To beat the storm, I tell him. Later, he asks if I'm still pushing them fast and if we're still beating the storm. Yes, I say, and so far — yes.

Between the questions, I'm thinking through our conversation with the florist, but then, mostly, I'm thinking about the scars on his arms — about the array of flesh tones revealed by fire, from white to pink to dark brown and every shade in between. I'm thinking about how it forever robs the skin of moisture and flexibility. How it tears through wrinkles, hair, and pores, around bellies, over genitals, how it fuses fingers and toes and leaves only a strange smoothness in its wake. How it transforms a body, turning it from red to gray to black and then you don't feel a thing.

I'm thinking about what fire does and about what fire did. I'm thinking about one quiet afternoon when I was nine years old, and about my own very personal encounter with the wholesale flesh-eater.

I had gone over to my best friend's house to pick him up and bring him back to mine. My mom was blanching and freezing a few dozen ears of corn for the winter, and he wanted to come over to help me eat through as many as we could get our hands on. His name was Keith. He was ten.

Keith was from a hard-core chore family. Every morning when I went to see him, he was slogging through a long list of jobs that often seemed much too involved for a ten-year-old. I was aware of it even as a kid. Keith was a son to his parents but he was also a burro, and sometimes they worked him like one they didn't care for much.

The afternoon I went to get him, he told me he was almost finished with his work and that he'd saved the best chore for last because he knew I was coming and that we could have fun with it. I looked through the list. The one job not crossed off read ominously *burn junk pile — use gas.* Off to the side of the house, behind a rusted topiary of Chevys and Fords, was a tall mountain of debris that included, among other things, a couch. Keith filled several one-gallon ice-cream pails to the rim with gasoline from an underground tank along the side of the garage. I still remember exactly what he said as the orange liquid sloshed into the second bucket, filling my head with its fumes — *one for the job and one for fun.* Even as a nine-year-old, I knew there was something quite wrong about an open pail of gasoline. I just didn't know how wrong.

Keith walked both pails over to the junk pile, setting one of them at the base and the other about ten feet away. Fumes bloomed from each bucket like image-distorting waves of heat — gasoline is always burning. I stood well back. I would have been right at Keith's shoulder if it weren't for the guilt of doing something wrong. I had an instinct that an open pail of gas would get me in trouble with my folks and told Keith as much, but he waved me off. *One for the job and one for fun.*

He threw the first pail into the air and it draped itself lovingly over the pile, setting the air above it shimmering. Keith asked with a wide smile if I'd ever seen a pail of gas go up, and I told him I hadn't. He pulled a farmer's match from his back pocket, drew it along the zipper of his fly, and tossed it at the pile. There was a mighty flash that seemed to come out of the middle of the heap rather than from the match. It made Keith duck, and then it made him laugh. I laughed too, but only because Keith did. The pile settled to a steady roar, and Keith turned for the second bucket.

I believe what he intended to do was spill a thin line of gas from the burning pile to the bucket, which he would leave partially full, so that a flame would burn along the ground and then go up in a plume when it hit. I'm only guessing, though, because the game was over a few seconds after it began. Keith leaned over the pail, spilling a line of gas that began about five feet from the burning pile. And then his life changed forever. The gas never touched the pile, but it didn't have to. In my memory the line catches fire in slow motion, but that's not at all how it happened.

As plain and as sure as a summer breeze, a wand of fire shot from the pile, swept through the air, raced up the line with amazing speed, and plunged straight into the bucket cradled in Keith's arms. A massive ball of fire simply appeared, followed by a penetrating *WHUP* and a wall of heat that blew straight through me. Keith was somewhere in the center of the ball, lost in a universe of fire that would, from that moment on, forever define him. For the rest of his life, that one ball of fire would be his story.

It lifted like a sideshow curtain and disappeared into a plume of black smoke. Keith emerged from underneath, covered with fire, running, stumbling, shouting. I told him to roll but don't think he'd have heard me if I had a bullhorn. I screamed it, but he screamed louder. I tried tripping him and then pushing him over, but he only ran.

It was the flames that finally laid him on the ground. He fell gradually, shaking his legs and pulling at the fire with his arms like it was something he might be able to slip out of. Very soon, he stopped moving altogether, and that's when I knew it was me or nothing. So I entered a kind of insanity, reaching straight into the flames to slap, batter, and pound every last one from his body.

When I was done, the fire was gone; Keith's body was smoking, the hair was burned off my arms and face, and the first seeds were planted in me that would grow up like a briar with thorns that ranged from bewilderment to rage, at the idea of a divine hand. Because if there was one, it hadn't seen fit to reach in and spare the two of us from something so horrible and so certain.

Keith had burned a long time. I'll not go into details about the smell or how it was to pull him from his clothes and lay him into a tub of cold water, because it's only gore. But it happened, and it's part of the memory and what I'm thinking on the road with my babies that brings me as coldly as I've ever arrived to the question: Where in hell was Keith's angel? I could try to believe I had an angel holding me safely back, but if that were true, then where was Keith's — a ten-year-old, eight months in the hospital with steel bars through his ankles to hold his legs up, and for the next year, walking with a cane in each hand, his legs moving like a marionette's. He fell so often I stopped noticing the cuts and bruises. He'd walk in from the playground with blood on his face like nothing more than a runny nose for all the attention it got. Where was his angel?

I'd gone back and forth over it ever since that awful afternoon. The deepest truth I could ever pull from the whole thing was angels up above or none at all — there is no mercy in a pail of gasoline.

Then Casey winds up and lets fly with a hard, fast one.

"Daddy, what is an *angel* mean?" It's been a year since the *what is dead mean?* on the same stretch of road, and the questions are not getting any easier.

"That man was talking about an angel, wasn't he —"

"But what *is* one, Dad?"

"Well —"

"— Yeah?" And because a child is always asking what you believe in, more than what you know, the question is, at its heart, the same as the florist's — do you believe in angels? Only for Casey, not knowing would not work, even if it was all I had.

"You know like what you put on top of a Christmas

tree?" I say, "That's an angel." Casey looks around at me with his eyebrows pushed down. Not an answer built to last — not what pulled the florist from his burning house and he knows it.

"But what do you *do* with one?"

"What do you do with an angel."

"Yeah, what — what is an angel *for*?"

"They're for making you feel better. Or they can make you feel safe. Like they made that man feel safe from a fire, even though he got burned. Did you see the way his arms were burned by the fire?"

"I remember."

"Well, you see, you always have to be very careful when you're around —"

"But, Dad — what does an angel look like?" Casey asks. And I'm so thoroughly unprepared for this, I can barely approach it, much less reach out and touch it. He presses relentlessly. "What did that man say — that angel was *glowing*?"

"Right, he said that, didn't he —"

"But why was he *glowing* for?"

"Well, Case, maybe we could ask the man if we see him again."

"That man was suppose to be dead?"

"I think he was talking about how the fire, Casey —"

"But why did he — why was he suppose to be dead?"

"Maybe if he — if the fire was too —"

"The man didn't die because of the angel?"

"Yes, that's what he said, isn't it."

"Because that angel helped him?"

"Right."

"Or else the man would be dead?"

"Yeah."

"And he's not worried any more?"

"I don't think he's worried."

"He's happy?"

"He looked happy."

We both fall silent, and I'm struck by an awareness like a light going on. Casey led me right into it. Keith. I think about him again but in a different way than all the other times I'd thought about him as a suffering, disfigured little boy. My memory had frozen him in time. Whenever he came to mind, I agonized over a boy who no longer existed. This time I thought about Keith as a man. We had fallen out of touch, but I'd heard he was married and had children. For all the times I asked myself where his angel was, I never acknowledged the fact that, just like the florist, Keith should be dead. He too should be buried in the mud. I was always so upset by the pain he endured and the damage to his body that I never counted the fact that he was still here.

I'm sure he does.

Pulled from the flames in the nick of time, he's alive today — somebody's husband, somebody's father, his parent's son. Probably not worried either. He might even look happy. And I'm only guessing here, but if he ever talks of angels, I bet the picture in his mind is of a young boy reaching in through a universe of fire to pull him free. An angel that looks just like me.

The anger I'd held for so long was suddenly lifted. The answer to the world's suffering hardly settled, but my own notes, like a suspended chord, finally resolved. I'm no fool to dodge a relief that's working — I'll take it with a cold glass of milk whenever it comes. Like a skillful teacher, Casey led me with his questions to the place that would make it right.

But he's not finished just yet. There's one more little detail that still needs attending.

"Dad?" he asks over the roar of a passing truck that seems to almost hit us even though it's well into the opposite lane. "Where does an angel live?"

"I — heaven. I guess."

"With God?"

"Sure, Casey, with God."

And he hands me a big iron padlock without a key and asks me to open it.

"But what *is* God?" An ancient old lock that countless generations have busted their hands and their best tools over and still not gotten apart. I remember sitting with one of my friends over a few beers, when both of our wives were pregnant, and asking him how he was going to handle the God question. Neither of us came up with anything worth mentioning. It seemed too far off to worry about. I thought that when the time came for an answer, I'd have come up with one I could live with. But I was wrong about that.

Casey pushes onward, not simply demanding that I enter the very mouth of mystery, requiring it. And as a parent you have to comply, with no more question than handing your child a slice of bread and a stick of cheese when he's hungry. With the first waves of rain beginning to fall in earnest, I search high and low for something to hang words on, but they only come crashing down around me. Every dead end only makes Casey push harder. In my head, I paddle wildly between truth and legend, religion and folklore — Incas, and Jesuits, and Rabbis — Oz, Zeus, Moses, Tecumseh, but the whole thing falls out of my mouth like bad ham.

By the time we reach the house, the ground all around us is boiling with rain. Owen wakes with a start as we are drenched in a matter of seconds. A strong wind races through the valley, setting off a chorus of banging doors and cracking limbs. Cows in the adjacent field bellow between claps of thunder. The head of the storm is nearly upon us. I roll us off the road and up the driveway, the metallic smell of ozone swirling through the air and deep into my chest as I huff the boys from the stroller. Under a glitter of lightning, I race up the walk with one under each arm. On the porch, the three of us strip out of our wet clothes and rush inside with the whole thing ripping at our heels.

The boys are wet and freezing, but the thrill of outrunning a storm rides high above any discomfort. Under wide smiles, their purple lips are shivering. Wet bangs stick to their foreheads as if drawn on with black marker. I pull a down comforter out of the closet and the three of us huddle together on the couch. The storm has muted us. Naked under the cover, we listen like forest animals.

Thunder blasts at the windows, and from either side of me the boys shoot their faces to mine. I pull them into my chest, but it's the glance at my eyes that gives them all they need to keep terror at bay. The storm is too violent for verbal assurances. I could tell them that thunder is nothing more than sound, that the house has stood for a hundred years against this and worse, but none of it would matter if they detected even a shred of concern in my eyes. What you say with words can be intellectualized — information can be faked. Children know this instinctively and will search through and around everything you ever tell them, to uncover not what you know, but what you believe. With a storm rocking the walls, belief trumps information every time.

Casey let me off the hook on identifying God as soon as the rain began drilling into our faces. Up to then I'd done my best, but there is no way around the fact that I'd failed completely. I'll have other chances to get it right. Casey has an unbelievably accurate filing system for all unanswered and poorly answered questions. He keeps track and he circles back. When this one rises again, I'll have to do better.

I'm envious of the florist and his unequivocal, straightforward belief that is not bound up with the complexity of what's real and what's metaphor. His angel was tall. It was beautiful, as all good angels should be. It was glowing. I want to give that kind of certainty to my sons, something simple and absolute for them to stand on — blue sky, brown earth, pink moon, and God in a long white beard on a great big chair.

If only I could believe it.

Despite having resolved the question of angels for myself, I can say nothing to Casey about God that comes anywhere close to being as real and palatable as a heavenly light in a burning building. But suddenly, I don't have to.

Like a dam giving way, the sky opens up and unleashes an explosion of thunder so powerful that it sets the walls shaking. The boys arch their bodies into my chest as the sound pours straight through and then all around us. The lowest frequencies roll and swell before spiking with impossible ferocity into a force that presses against our skin with an actual presence. For a moment, there is only sound, its immense power engulfing all that resides with it. And for that moment, we are gone. Disappeared. For that moment, we are one with it.

Then back, and the boys looking into my face. The sound trails off, but something is left in its place, like the glow in your arm after a good hard blow. There is something else in the room with us — immensely powerful as it is delicately tender; the sky ripping open, the blaze of lightning, the crushing wind, but also under the blanket in the chill that leaves our bodies, the feeling of getting warmer, the closeness of our skin, and the perfect song that Owen sings again. Casey smiles up at me with the awareness of this thing in the room. And he has his answer — as wordless and certain as his brother's song.

I don't need to tell him what God is. The answer is all around us. Revealed only when I stopped binding it with language, it lies just beyond what can ever be spoken — one of the mysteries that begin to crack open when all talking is set aside.

Words are strangers to Casey and enemies to Owen — they both rely on something quite different to make sense of the world, something that can only be described as knowing. Something that works quite brilliantly even though we adults have almost completely stopped using it — stopped believing that it is possible to deeply know something that can never be explained. And Casey will know these things — he will know the pounding skies and he will know God. He will know the softness of his brother's voice and he will know angels.

THE KISS

Owen's kisses are painful on the receiving end.

More like head butts than any show of affection as he leans in, usually without warning, and bounces his forehead against my nose or eyeball. Each one is a non sequitur, springing from origins that have nothing to do with what's going on around him. I've gotten so I can catch the look in his face like a love-drunk pirate as the desire wells up in him and overflows into a crashing blow. But if I'm not watching when the feeling hits him, if he's on my hip while I'm on the phone or waiting to cross the street or about to bite into a sandwich — *bang,* he fires his mantle like a tiny ball of iron, straight at my head. I try to receive them in the spirit they're given, but it doesn't change the fact that they're blindside hits, and painful.

For what they lack in their delicacy, they more than make

up for with their sincerity. As adults, we make the kiss a serving platter for an array of intentions — a means to an end that often has very little to do with anything in the vicinity of affection. It starts early in life. I remember the pin-prick, wake-up-it's-time-to-go-to-school kisses my mom used to deliver like cups of coffee each morning, followed by the be-good-and-make-me-proud kisses I carried like weights on the way out the door. The smothering peace-be-with-you kisses in church. Then, when you get older, you get the hang of it with the baby-I'm-sorry-I-was-out-all-night kiss at four A.M. with your coat still on to your lover in bed. And the please-can-I-have-this-thing-I-don't-really-deserve kisses that fly back and forth like gnats in most relationships. Or the flat, lifeless I'm-leaving-for-work-and-if-we-don't-do-this-we'll-slowly-grow-apart kiss exchanged between spouses each morning like money at a register. In a world of ulterior motive kisses, Owen's are sweet with the clarity of pure adoration.

Casey's first kisses were different, every bit as unpredictable, although the tariff wasn't as steep when you didn't see them coming. Usually when I least expected it, he'd open his mouth and bob it against whatever part of my body that was closest. I could be neck deep in the middle of anything at all and look down to find his head bouncing against my knee, his eyes looking up, glowing with fondness.

As nice as these first kisses were, they pale in comparison to what the boys reserve for Susan. When it comes to the truest displays of affection, they have always saved the real thing for their mother. They eat their mother. There is no other way to put it. They throw her to the floor and make a meal of her. She's a peach pie à la mode reduced to tears of laughter as they swab her with their muzzles, gnawing her ears, drooling into her neck. I worry that one day one of them will walk off with her chin in his mouth.

"They do this to you during the day?" she asks one afternoon, defending herself against an onslaught of affection. Just home from work with her coat still on and she's tackled and slathered, the boys mouthing her face as if it were covered with honey.

"Yeah, they get me," I say halfheartedly as they twist their arms into her hair. She throws me her sunglasses and keys. "Not really like that but —"

"It's because I'm gone all day," she says and then yelps and tells them to be gentle.

"We wrestle, you know," I say, but she's not really listening. "Owen usually just smashes his head into my face when he wants to show me how much he cares."

Casey does a roundhouse, Owen circles him for a gravity assist, and then they're both lying across her face. She bucks the pin, comes up laughing, and suddenly the idea of children making you young again isn't just a dumb thing people say, because the wrinkle in her nose and the rise of her eyebrows are like I haven't seen since she was eighteen.

Kisses fly like breezes through this house. And just like breezes, their paths can be hard to predict. Every thousandth one or so conspires with circumstances around it to become something unusual. Hot meets cold and they agree to a spiral dance, the sky turns purple, the mood is right, and what began as a kiss turns into a force that blows the roof off.

———

I'm high up in the rafters of the barn, scaling the hand-hewn framework like a spider on a giant wooden web. It's a cold Saturday morning in October; breath shoots from my mouth and nose in aerosol bursts. I've been gazing at these beams and meaning to get up in them for the past year. Old barns hold their talismans in the rafters, and I'm looking to find what's held up in this one. After an hour of scavenging, I've gathered a cupboard collection worthy of the most discriminating New England witch — a porcelain doorknob, a brass name plate, a bundle of oak pegs, seven wrought-iron hinges, a wooden pulley, a clock, a tongue-and-groove box of iron nails, two locks with their skeleton keys, an ax, a sickle, three chains, two animal skulls, and a snuffbox. There's more, some intriguing dark shapes in the corners of the roofing supports, but I'm as high as my nerves will take me.

While I'm up, I decide to remove the planks lying across the main center beams so that when I walk in I can see the pegged-oak framing that makes an old barn like no other structure on earth. I heave the first plank over the edge of a beam and it cascades to the floor, twirling off years of grime in spiral streamers and crashing to the ground in a heavy cloud of dust. Several more and the roof above begins to open up, the sun streaking through to the floor from high above with cathedral-like solemnity.

Susan comes by, her eyebrows pushed low, probably caught by the sound of falling boards, some of them smashing into splinters when they hit. She's with her sister, who's carrying her six-month-old in a frontpack. Casey and Owen race in from behind them and come to a dead stop beneath me. I have to quit what I'm doing or risk sawing them in half. For a moment, they all squint up at me as if I'm a sideshow moron. Even the six-month-old.

"What on earth are you doing up there?" Susan finally asks. She's not exactly reprimanding, but there's reprimand in the tone, there's reprimand in the expression. And in her stance — legs wide, a hand on the hip and the other over her eyes as she looks twenty-five feet up to the soles of my boots.

"Just throwing boards around," I say, trying to make throwing boards around sound like a casual thing. Her reprimanding stance is unwavering. "These boards are blocking the view of the ceiling," I say. "I just want to — I've been meaning to move them ever since we got here." She is far from impressed. The collective look on their faces says it all — you'll break your neck, you big idiot. Even the six-month-old.

"It looks dangerous up there," Susan says.

"Just a lot of noise," I say. The boys are tottering around below me.

"Why is Daddy throwing boards for?" Casey asks plainly.

"I don't know why Daddy's up there," she says as a way of saying it to me.

"That's the kind of thing it's just better not to watch," her sister says softly. She turns and leaves.

"Are those beams strong enough to hold you?" Susan asks without moving.

"Sure," I say. "Could you move the guys? I only have a couple more." She gathers them under her arms, and moves back. I throw another one down. It spirals grime, bangs mightily against the floor and breaks apart.

"This is so you can see the ceiling when you walk in here?" she asks, making it sound ridiculous. The next board is large. I have to bring my center of gravity low against the beam I'm on as I whirl it around and heave it over. It lands with a loud smash. Susan hates it. "Is there bat dung on those planks?"

"Probably a little bit of everything."

"That bat dung is bad to breathe you know," she says and allows Casey to run back underneath me.

"Is this all right with you?" I ask, rising from my crouch, a little upset for having to get permission.

"I just love you, that's all," she says with the hand still on her hip. But she means it. She calls the boys back to her, telling them to let me finish. Casey picks up a board with a jagged point at the end of it and charges off.

Several more planks and then I'm on the ground clearing the debris out of the walkway and into a pile I'll do something with later. The trick with having a barn when you're not a farmer is to keep from filling it to the rim with piles of debris that you'll do something with later. A nonworking farm is a junk magnet. Back home in Wisconsin, I always knew the farmers who went bankrupt by the condition of their barnyards. Working farms run clean. Even if they look haphazard, every object has a purpose. But when the number of vehicles on blocks outside the milk house reaches seven, that's a farmer in trouble.

Casey comes racing around the corner with the pointed board shouldered like a .30-.30. He aims it in my direction and charges, showing no signs of slowing as he closes in. I tell him to stop just before he impales my side with it.

"Why?" he asks.

"Because that will hurt if you poke me with it," I say. He turns and runs from the barn and around the corner. Soon, I hear Susan admonishing — *"No, no, Casey. Not with Owen."* And then again — *"Hey, Casey, that's not very nice — you'll hurt Owen."* I feel my temper flash as I imagine him pushing the point into his little brother. I leave what I'm doing and round the corner just in time to see him lunging the old splintered thing into Susan's legs. She pushes him away. Asks him to be good. He turns from her and runs in my direction, the board held above him like a javelin. Our eyes meet. I say his name. He knows better but runs it into me anyway. Softly, but he does run it into me. He has no concept of my discomfort or he's outright trying to hurt me. It's no good either way. The tip of the board breaks against my jeans.

"It's mine now," I say, sounding so like an adult and even more like a parent. He holds onto it. "Give it to me," I say slowly. He doesn't. I take hold of it and pull, but he holds tight with one hand. His face is calm, watching now. I crouch toward him. I lower my voice to keep it from spiking and tell him to let go of the board. He shuts his eyes. I say his name. I jerk it. He holds tight. Then I do something I would have never imagined possible. I hit him. I slap him, very hard, on the top of his hand.

He releases the board instantly, his face growing long with shock as though I've not just slapped his hand but gone and cut it off. I win. The board *is* mine. When it gets down to the wire, the game between parent and child is never really a contest. It's a rigged fight. The parent always wins. Even when the obedience feels cheap. Even when it feels like it could bend under its own weight.

"Why did you hit me?" he asks, bewildered. I'm about to try an answer but the quiver in his bottom lip makes everything that comes to mind sound stupid. "You hurt me," he says plainly. "You hurt my hand, Daddy." He holds it like it burns but he's too overwhelmed to cry. His eyes are searching for meaning. He wants to understand why I stepped out of bounds, why I brought out such a big hammer and used it so decisively. Only a slap on the hand, but the impact on him is as if I'd all-out clobbered him — his reaction the same as if I'd broken his arm, so the fact that I haven't is a minor detail. The emotion pouring from his face is a different color than any I've seen before. From that one slap. It makes me want to take it back.

I leave him to Susan, who has seen the whole thing, and carry the board back to the barn. Just as my head is filling with justifications — *can't poke people with a stick, being a good parent is no popularity contest, a child has to listen, a parent has to be firm,* Casey comes running around the corner, still on the verge of tears, with his lower lip bouncing.

"Kiss it," he says, holding his hand out to me. His eyes are astonished, desperate. I'm still emboldened, my defenses wearing like armor — *a spoiled child is a miserable child, a soft parent is a lazy parent.* He steps closer and lifts his hand. The skin on top is rose-colored and full. I take it in mine and turn it over, brushing a shallow silver from his palm. He turns it back and raises it to my face.

"Kiss it, Daddy," he pleads, tears brimming in his eyes. I lower to my knees and put his hand to my lips. I kiss him and something profound happens — my anger vanishes, my defenses melt away and are replaced with a shame I've never felt before.

Casey's lip stops shaking. His shoulders lower. "Why did you hurt me, Daddy?" he asks, his eyes smooth and gray like a lake after a storm. I lean into his cheek with my head down, because I can't look at him.

"I was mad because you wouldn't let go of the board," I say. He backs away from me so he can look into my face. "I'm sorry, Casey. I'm sorry I hurt you." And I know as soon as the words fall from my mouth, that this is something I've said for myself. Casey doesn't need my sorrow. And he won't forgive me either, he doesn't know how — at his age, forgiveness doesn't apply. I search his face, and there's not a trace of anger there. He holds no grudge and will give no pardon. Both eyes are filled to the rim with his only desire: for the two of us to be right again. Nothing else matters.

He holds his fingers to my lips and I kiss again. This time my head swims with emotion as I'm asked to mend what I had so recently broken. I feel his hand even though it's his heart I'm holding. He trusts me with it so suddenly after I broke it. He gives it to me because somehow he knows that the only one who can truly repair the damage is the one who caused it. And it makes me wonder how different my life would be if, so suddenly, I had to kiss everything I had ever broken. If I had to mend every heart I had ever wronged.

Susan is watching. She turns when I see her but not quickly enough to hide the red rims of her eyes. Casey backs away, and he's fine now. He takes his hand from me and skips out of the barn — no strings attached, no lingering anger.

I watch him run down the gradual hill to the house and wonder when it was that I forgot how to do that? How long ago did I lose track of that perfection? Without a single word, he made me understand the pain I had caused by bringing it to my face and pressing it to my lips.

The sun peers through nail holes in the roof and rains down around me in tiny spotlights. I look up through the rays like I did as a child when the blue and red light passed through the stained-glass windows of my old school. And just like that school back then, this old barn seems to hold me. I retreat to a quiet spot near the back, by an old stone wall. The lesson is fresh; I have to study it before it scabs over. And in my mind, I roll through images of loved ones in the past who wronged me and imagine how differently things might have turned out if, instead of lashing back or shutting them out, I'd had the wisdom of a child and the courage to simply ask for a kiss.

THE RINK

It all started with the cat.

The cat was nice. A black barn cat named C. R. I have no idea what the letters stand for. Friends of ours were moving and couldn't take him, so they asked us if he could stay in our barn. He's a mouser, they said. They gave us his feeding regimen, his rabies and distemper schedules, a cat carrier, told us his likes and dislikes and said that he'd spray the couches the first chance we gave him. I forgot to ask about the name. Anyway, C.R. seemed to fit just right in a home with boys named K. C. and O. N. Really not too sure how that happened, though.

C. R. came with a much younger and more cat-like tabby named Maggie, who bit much of her fur off on the drive over and never found our barn quite appealing enough despite numerous cans of tuna. In our only family picture with her, she's looking off in the distance, planning her escape.

One day, she disappeared. C. R. stayed, and C. R. was nice. From the moment he stepped inside the barn, he loved it as much as I did. He follows us like a Lab on walks through the forest, and doesn't jump on the picnic plates; I don't know about the mouser, but he keeps the raccoons, possums, and groundhogs in the woods where they belong.

Then there was the goldfish from the county fair that was supposed to die after twenty-four hours, only nobody told him. The neighbor girl gave him to the boys because she'd won something like ten of them at the Ping-Pong ball toss. She gave us two, actually, and the second one lived up to his end of the deal — he didn't last long. Casey named that one Maker for some reason, and it doomed him. Maker didn't make it. Never name an animal Maker. If you want something to last forever, name it Otto.

Otto the fish is still alive, three years and several out-of-water experiences after Maker's demise. He's outlived three subsequent fair-prize goldfish, and his odd stamina shows no signs of fading. It has to be something in the name. I'm thinking about using it for Susan and the boys as well as for several good friends and relatives as a way of securing their future.

The first real break in the animal dam was the rabbit. Because once you get a rabbit, really, what's to stop you from getting just about any other animal under the sun. This might be hard to understand if you don't actually own a rabbit. The thing is, if you're not going to haul off and eat it one afternoon, then it's really not *for* anything. A rabbit doesn't exactly radiate affection. Holding one that's full-grown can be difficult. You can't bait a hook with one. They don't lay eggs. You can always look at them and that's okay, but you can look at a picture of one and get roughly the same effect if you imagine the nose twitching.

Susan brought the rabbit home one afternoon, Casey promptly named him Mermaid, and he was a member of the family before we were even formally introduced.

"What is this?" I asked, stepping out of the truck and up the walkway to find the big black thing sitting next to Casey and Owen on the lawn.

"You've never seen one of these?" Susan asked with a smirk. "They're called rabbits."

"Right. What's it doing in our yard?"

"He's Mermaid," Casey said.

Susan smiled warmly. "The boys named him Mermaid."

"A male rabbit named Mermaid?"

"The third-grade teacher at my school just married a man who's opposed to it."

"He's opposed to rabbits."

"She keeps it in her classroom during the week but has to take it home on weekends and holidays, and he doesn't want it peeing all over their house."

"Can you believe the kind of jerks some people marry?"

"We could keep him in the small barn, Marc. It will be nothing."

"You think he'll fit in there?"

"Do I think he'll fit in the barn?"

"He's big — look at him, he's huge. A rabbit is not supposed to dwarf a child. He's like a prehistoric rabbit. He's like a carnivorous — like a meat-eating carnivorous rabbit."

"It's a special kind that gets big."

"Well, sure it is . . . and I can see why Casey named him Mermaid," I said. "That has to be on the shortlist of names for gigantic black male rabbits."

"Well, what do you think, should we keep him?" Susan asked and Casey chimed as if cued by a director. "Yeah — can we keep him, Dad? Please, can we keep him?"

"As if I have a choice?"

"C'mon, it'll be fun."

"I don't want to be the one who always feeds him."

"Fine, Marc. So you're up for it?"

"Think we can change his name to Maker?"

The dog was inevitable. We knew as soon as we moved in that the place needed a dog as much as it needed a paint job. Friends visiting from the city would ask where the dog was as if the house were lacking a front door and windows until we got one. So when we went to Wisconsin to visit Susan's parents and her father's best dog had just given birth to puppies and they were the special German shorthair/ Brittany mix he'd developed over the past twenty years, it was difficult not to leave with the whole litter. We watched them tumbling under their mother's swollen teats, trying to imagine which one might best walk the fine line between iron brute and love machine. The boys picked out a brown-faced male and dropped him on his head; he came running back for more.

"There he is," I said.

We brushed him off, looked him over, and tried to think of a name. For as long as Susan can remember, all of her dad's male dogs have been Duke and all the females have been Belle. We couldn't think of anything strong enough to break the tradition, so we named the puppy after his father. Susan's dad never thought of it as a question.

"You takin' a Duke or a Belle?" he hollered from the house as we plopped the pup into a box and placed it on the backseat of the truck between the boys.

"A Duke," I hollered back. "We got a Duke."

The quail came with the Christmas tree. Four of them. They don't eat much.

We go to a cut-your-own tree farm on a huge tract of land toward the end of the valley. They give you a saw at the little stand when you drive in, and for fifteen dollars you can cut down any tree you're able to haul out. I hiked into the forest to cut one down while Susan stayed back with the boys, who were more interested in a cage full of wild turkeys than a walk through the pines. Twenty minutes later, I came back dragging a tree and found Susan talking to the owner.

"Wife here tells me you got a pointer," he said as I approached.

"It's true."

"Well, by-golly."

"Yup —"

"You got him under any birds yet?"

"He's only about six months."

"Well, hey, he's ready — let me get'cha a few."

We loaded the cage into the pickup and put the tree on top. Susan and the boys informed me on the drive home that the quail were our new friends and would not be chased through the woods by the dog. I bought a waterer and a fifteen-pound bag of game feed that afternoon.

Now unless you've actually seen a small flock of them casually scratching the ground at sunrise, it will probably be hard to understand why we got the chickens. I realize there's a large portion of the population more than willing to write you off at the mere sound of crowing in your yard. I used to be one of them. And I'm the first to admit that the chicken is a hard animal to respect. They defecate in their food, eat their own eggs, trample their young, and peck each other's eyeballs — not the first things you look for in an animal for the family.

But one morning while I was standing outside a neighbor's house, a small flock of them came scratching over, and I was forced to rethink my prejudice against them as dumb and plain. Something about these was different. "They're bantams," the lady of the house told me. "Fully developed chickens in miniature. They're friendlier than regular chickens — watch, they'll walk right up to you. There's not much on them for eating, but we like them because of the colors. They're good layers and they keep the ticks down."

"They eat ticks?" I asked.

"They sure do," she said proudly. "There ain't a tick on this property."

Small, colorful, egg-laying, tick eaters. Suddenly I needed at least twelve. The woman gave me the address of the man who had given her the ones scratching around our feet, and I introduced myself to him that afternoon. He smiled over the hood of my truck as I made my request — yes, he could spare a few bantams, and yes, he could catch them for me, and no, he wouldn't take money for them.

"Don't even know how many I got back here. I just keep 'em for the ticks," he said. "They eat ticks."

"Do they," I said.

"They sure do."

"Ticks go in and eggs come out," I said dumbly. "Pretty good deal." He smiled, looking back to the boys strapped in their car seats, and I wondered what he secretly thought about a grown man with his children in the middle of the day running around looking for chickens. That night, he gave us a rooster and two hens. The following week, I found a place that sold chicks. I bought twelve.

Susan was unsure about the prospect of having chickens, but the old-timers in their overalls standing around the counter at the Agway Pet and Farm all agreed that I'd done the right thing.

"Pretty little birds," one said.

"The boys will love them," said another.

"They'll hatch them eggs if you don't get 'em quick," said one against the wall.

And then a guy by the telephone, with a quick shake of his head — "Best mothers on the planet, them little banties."

A man brought out my fifty-pound bag of egg-layer mash and twenty-pound bag of scratch corn. He heaved them onto the counter and leaned in, his eyes barely showing under the dirty rim of his cap — "Had a buddy wid a couple a dem banties," he said slowly. "Weren't a tick on his property."

Now that we've had them for the past year, I finally understand what the animal downpour was all about. While it was happening, I told myself it was a random thing, that there was nothing more to it than getting a rhubarb from the neighbor and putting it in the ground — an empty patch of dirt and you stick a plant in, an empty hutch on the side of the barn and you fill it with the world's largest rabbit. We got a couple of animals, I told friends, no reason — just enjoy having them around.

Now I know there was more to it than that. There was a plan, the very existence of which represented a sort of denial. Each animal, with its ceaseless need to be fed, watered, cleaned, and then simply looked at, was a way of postponing the inevitable. A way for me to avoid the noisy, brightly colored, over-the-top play palaces catering exclusively to children. I was naive to think a quiet barnyard of animals could keep me from this — that I could fill my son's days with pleasant hobby-farm chores and call it a childhood. No matter how many creatures we got, after the boys and I cleaned their pens, collected their eggs, and filled the food trays, we were always confronted by this relentless thing called *the rest of the day*. And despite the fact that Casey and Owen had thrilled over the way a chick hides between your fingers when you hold it, and the sound a quail makes like sneakers against a gym floor, they'd both reached the point where they needed to know if there was anything more to life than this.

When that feeling hits them, you can see it like a color in their eyes. Only the most uncaring parent wouldn't drop everything and put his own aesthetic aside to enter the blazingly colorful, buzzing and dinging, clown-faced, hokey music world of children's playlands. Here in Cherry Valley, no self-respecting parent would deny a child the heady pleasure of a visit to the Rink.

It's Wednesday, and the boys are out of their minds with anticipation. We talked about it the night before, and they woke up with it singing on their lips: we're going to the roller rink. They have no idea what that means but somehow know it will be better than throwing cracked corn at chickens. Wednesday is advertised as "kiddie jamboree" day. The rink is closed to all skaters from nine until noon so that kiddies six and under can bring out anything with wheels and get it on. After a hasty breakfast, we load a trike into the back of the truck and head out.

This rink, like so many roller rinks for some reason, is on the outskirts of town where you'd expect rock quarries and trucker bars to be. As we draw near, a large plywood sign with two crudely painted skaters informs us we're only a mile away. The landscape begins to deteriorate. Along the road, the sun is falling through the trees as if from God's own hand, but pockets of desperation smolder all around us — in front lawns strewn with broken toys and rusted medical equipment, under streetlamps with their globes shattered, between the lines of a towering billboard that reads with menacing exclamation marks, *GOT A JOB?!!!*

GET A CAR!!! I try not to take it as an omen. We arrive with me explaining to the boys just exactly what a roller rink is all about — even though I haven't the slightest idea of what we're in for.

I turn the truck into an enormous lot that is mostly empty. Parked near the entrance, a colorful necklace of shining minivans seem to practically scream in unison: there are mothers here, lots and lots of mothers. I feel a pull in my stomach, like an uninvited wedding guest. They will all know each other. They will have shopped for clothing at the same stores, caught the same sales, ordered from the same catalogs. They will have discussed their plantings, from bulb to vine to flowering bush. They will have exchanged the very meat loaf and meringue recipes their own mothers exchanged a generation before them. There will be pearls and some heels, snapping gum, and the smell of nail polish. There will be extensions. There will be acrylic tips. I haven't even stepped foot inside, and I already feel like I should leave.

"Three-fifty for the boys," the woman says behind bullet-proof-thickness Plexiglas. She's in her mid-fifties, overweight, and filling the small booth generously. Muffled children's music thumps on the other side of the heavy black doors to her right. A sign hung above in black painted letters reads NO METAL TRIKES. "That yours?" the woman asks, nodding toward the metal trike around my arm. I tell her it is. "You bringing it in?" she asks. I tell her I'd like to. She takes a long breath and shakes her head as if I told her I also like to rob banks. I want to tell her that as a father, perhaps the only real difference between me and the mothers on the other side of the thumping doors is that I can't bring myself to buy plastic playthings. One look at my stroller says it all. It's a failing, I admit it. Our toy box is filled with toe breakers and stitches makers — I'm the one to blame for the cast-iron tractors, the steel trains, the stamped metal trucks.

"I'll watch him with it," I say, and the woman nods dismissively with a look in her eyes that says, *whadya expect from a father* . . . like every mother in America instinctively knows right down to her Wonder Bra — for God's sake, man, you don't bring a metal trike to a roller rink.

I pay the lady and drag the boys through the turnstile. The black doors swing open, and the three of us are transported into a seventies time lock.

Ceiling-mounted domes of colored lights spin slowly. The walls are striped with black lights. An enormous mirror ball showers us with its glitter. The look on Casey's face is like I've walked him through the psychedelic gates of heaven. Owen isn't as sure. I wade them through a sea of children, and we plop down on a large maroon shag-covered circular bench near a lit-up case of skating and martial arts trophies. Casey makes a beeline for the rink as soon as I get his coat off. He sets his trike down on the vast blue surface and motors off to join the rest of the kids rolling madly around on every wheeled vehicle imaginable. Owen is quite happy to stay in my arms. With the mad ruckus practically engulfing us in its frenzy, I'm quite happy to hold him. You'd need a search-and-rescue team to find a lost kid in this place. We make it out to the center of the rink, and I race to keep up with Casey and his outlaw trike so I can keep them from causing any major injuries.

I do a quick scan on the first go-round. The rink is like a hooker who cleaned herself up for a morning with children. All the spinning lights and hokey music can't hide the true spirit of the place, which seeps through in the smell like a party on the morning after, the stacks of highball glasses filled with cigarette butts hidden in the corners. Casey is wheeling around full bore. His small shoulders are tight up against his neck. His eyebrows are frozen at the top of his forehead. His mouth is stuck in a wide, happy grimace. His legs are a blur. The older children know well enough to steer around him. Some glance over their shoulders as they pass, giving Case a well-deserved look as they do. He barrels on unaware, using the children he approaches as obstacles, steering around them as close as he can. I dive at his rear wheels just as he's about to ram into the back of a beautiful little girl on a pink horse. I bend down and tell him to be careful, but he can't see me for the lights in his eyes — the happy grimace molded to his face. Suddenly the no-metal-trikes rule makes perfect sense.

Another scan on the second go-round. Not a father in the place. One guy, but I can't quite make him out. He smiles and gives me the *hey — we're both guys* look as he passes, but he's a little too good on the skates for me to feel like running up and slapping his shoulder. A grown man with tassels on his laces, he holds his legs tightly together on the turns, hopping backward and then forward, his arms fluttering like a bird, and you can almost hear the way the girls must have gone for it in his old high school days.

On the sidelines, a clutch of mothers look on as their toddlers beat the tar out of a Baywatch pinball machine. A large group just down from them huddles together, their shoulders bobbing under a din of high laughter. They look up when I pass, regarding me politely. Behind mannerly smiles, their eyes cast doubt — *there is something wrong with him — he's lost his job, his wife works at a drive-thru. Could be he's a widower or maybe a divorcé without the good sense to leave the children where they'd be better off, with their mother.*

We round the back wall and race headlong into "The Mural" — the primitively rendered postadolescent, hodge-podge collage, a version of which has to exist in just about every small-town roller rink across the county: flat-finish black paint, over which are hand-painted images of old rock stars, planets, galaxies, big-chested blonds in tight shirts, muscle cars, fighter planes, lightning bolts, and, of course, skaters — some holding hands, some dancing, others kissing, although this seems to be a difficult activity to depict in fluorescent tempera. The painter seems to have started with the locked lips, but given up completely by the time he reached the foreheads, which look fused together.

Samuel Wright is singing "Under the Sea," and as I chase Casey over the rink's vast blue surface, it has never sounded more fitting. The song rumbles out of giant stage speakers better suited for the local garage band's version of "Stairway to Heaven" than to Disney's *Little Mermaid.*

The music stops suddenly, and the female equivalent of Mr. Tassels comes skating into the middle of the rink holding a wireless mike. "Hokey-pokey time," she cheers, but her voice sounds tired. "Hokey-pokey time, boys and girls." The crowd knows exactly what this cry means. Casey, Owen, and I watch as they push the wheeled toys off the rink and gather in a large circle around the woman. We follow their lead and join in the circle. The work lights on the rink are bumped up to their full brightness. The effect is like closing time at a bar, when you can see everything and everybody more clearly and nothing is as clean or as beautiful as it had seemed.

The woman in the center waits for the group to form, skating casually forward and backward on one skate and then the other. She was started on skates at a young age. You can tell. As the last of the children and mothers file into the circle, she has her head down, concentrating through the steps of a dance routine, silently mouthing the words to a song, and it's suddenly apparent that this is the kind of woman who is more comfortable around a circle of lights than a circle of children. You get the feeling that this is just a day job — that she really comes alive as the Xanadu roller queen at night.

The needle drops on a record and bumps loudly over the speakers.

"Turn it down, Marty," the woman barks toward the DJ booth at the far end of the rink. "A little more, a little more," she says, with the music starting. And then the whole circle breaks into the hokey-pokey, with the woman calling out the moves and doing them so we can follow along.

Susan would be so much better at this.

The music echoes and blurs through the rink. Some children are smiling, but many are staring into space as their mothers throw their arms and legs around as the song tells them. I freeze. Not a reaction I would have predicted, but suddenly it's crystal clear: for me, the hokey-pokey is not possible. I just can't do it. Not because I'm better than the hokey-pokey, not because I think the hokey-pokey is a dumb thing or that it means anything about who you are if you do the hokey-pokey. I can't do it because it's just not in me. The funky chicken, maybe. Not the hokey-pokey. This is something you can only know about yourself when the music is flowing all around you and the roller queen is demanding that you put your right hip in. It's like a street fight — you don't know how you're going to react until you're there.

By the middle of the song, with the mothers "shaking it all about" and "turning themselves around," I feel like the last person wearing clothes at a nude beach — as if the roller queen is about to bear down on her mike — *Hey, pal, you can't just stand there and watch — you do the hokey-pokey or you hit the road.*

I look around at the circle of mothers moving themselves and their children's bodies to the music, and I'm suddenly struck by the question, exactly who is doing what for whom here? Is anybody doing this because they want to? On their own, children don't hokey-pokey. The mothers are a game bunch, but I can't see them breaking into a quick version in the parking lot just for laughs. The roller queen would rather be necking, but the dance is going strong. The children are doing it for their mothers, the mothers are doing it for their children, the woman in the center is doing it for all of us, and I'm feeling like I have to do it for all of them.

The pressure to join in is intense. The song is endless. My grin has worn out. There's no leaving now. I have to hokey-pokey or fake a seizure.

I turn to Owen — the youngest is always the easiest target. I put his right hip in. His little face grows concerned. I "shake him all about" and "turn him all around," but then he's just clamoring for me to hold him. Casey gives me a "don't even try it" look, and I know it's my fault. I've ruined it for them — *whadya expect from a father*. They'll never hokey-pokey like normal children.

Later, somewhere in the middle of the limbo, it hits me as never before — the fact that Casey and Owen are spending an enormous amount of time with their father. For the first time since they were born, I'm wondering if that's okay, because the mothers are enthusiastically shimmying back and under the bar to the booming echo from the loudspeakers and because I can't bring myself to limbo either.

The roller queen holds one end of the bar and someone in a large yellow dinosaur costume holds the other end. Casey and Owen give it a tentative try after I encourage them, and soon they're racing under the bar with the rest of the children. I'm relieved that they can enjoy it without me. For reasons I could never fully explain, I'd rather hokey-pokey on a bed of coals than limbo wildly in front of these strangers, the yellow dinosaur cheering me on.

Suddenly, with every child except Casey and Owen running under the bar with mother in tow, my mind is racing through all of the things not just Susan but many other women do with their children — things I'm not doing with mine. Homemade Play-Doh, Duck Duck Goose, nursery rhymes, long morning snuggles, "Twinkle Twinkle Little

Star," "This Old Man," "Itsy Bitsy Spider," and all the rest. What happens when children are deprived of their daily dose of "Itsy Bitsy Spider"? Except for weekends and weekday evenings when Susan's not wiped out from work, the boys get little of it. What they get is their father, midweek, midday, on the dark side of a rink with his hands in his pockets. I'm better than this. I know it's true, but at the moment it doesn't seem like it.

I remember how proud of my mother I always felt when we'd go out — a big wave of hair around her pretty face and just the right outfit. I wonder how I'd have felt if it were my father instead — what about him would have made me as proud. As I look back on it, I can see that I always thought highly of my dad for what he did, and highly of mom for who she was. Could my boys ever be proud of a dad for who he is? — even when their friends ask what he does and they can only answer: he points out the bear tracks in the forest and will limbo for no one?

My dad swears to this day that with all things pertaining to parenting, my mother has him beaten hands down. If that's true, is she better at it because she's a woman? Is it possible that even the best man is ever really cut out for raising children? Do women possess an inherent patience, skill, and willingness to hokey-pokey that just makes them better? Or are they superior to men just because they do it more?

They do it differently. At the moment, this is overwhelmingly apparent.

The bar goes low, and the mothers are bending forward to get under instead of backward. They all see this as very funny for some reason, and I'm feeling critical now, knowing full well that it's no more than a hybridized strain of sour grapes, one of the guerrilla tactics of maintaining self-esteem when you're completely outnumbered — if you can't join 'em, beat 'em.

I have to be critical, because admitting the truth is so much harder — that at this moment, the mothers are better. That in this world, I will never quite cut it. That if only by virtue of the fact that full-time mothers are the overwhelming majority, I will always run a distant second. Forget whether or not Susan as a woman is an intrinsically better parent. This is a simple game of numbers — a majority membership is something most children will kill to have. It's like the parents who opt for circumcision not because it's better but because they don't want their child to feel different from his peers in the showers. Right now, I'm thinking about my boys in the lunchroom — forget showers, forget circumcision — how are they going to feel in front of their friends when they open a bag and pull out a sandwich that was made by their father?

After the limbo, the kids all race to secure a booth in the hot dog and soda fountain shop just off the far corner of the rink. I move the boys with the crowd, and soon we're eating like the rest of them — except for the fact that I'm the only one sitting with my kids. The mothers are gathered into comfortable-looking chat circles that instantly bring me back to grade-school playground days, where the only thing more ruthless than a tight huddle of girls was a hornet's nest.

One of the women breaks away from the group and comes over to introduce herself to me and make nice comments about the boys. She is very kind. Her eyes are large and listening, and she laughs generously at everything I say. But then she nods her head a little too vigorously as I'm speaking, and I suddenly have a feeling of what it's like to be disabled, what it's like to be *special*.

The yellow dinosaur passes through the booths pretending to steal children's hot dogs. He tries our table, but the boys are hungry and don't see the humor. Only as he hops away, do I notice that the man in the tasseled skates has been mysteriously absent. The dinosaur's hop has a certain flair that seems familiar. Just coincidence? You decide.

The *Little Mermaid* sound track is back on full. Ariel is wailing through "A Whole New World," which also seems madly fitting. Only I'm much less sure of my whole new world than she is of hers. I have a feeling, somehow, that my former life is still out there. Somewhere there are people drinking merlot into the sunset, gasping at Lucian Freud paintings, marveling at a Laurie Anderson concert, reading Harry Crews with a whisky.

It strikes me as I'm sitting under the spinning lights with a bad hot dog in my mouth that from the moment I stepped foot into this place I've been experiencing a kind of progressive breakdown, and it's reached the point where I no longer know exactly who I am. There's kryptonite in the walls. I'm feeling weak. I've lost track of what I'm doing. There are magnets behind the mirrors. Grease on the lens. I don't know why I'm here. Smoke in the hallway. This place is no good for me. I let Casey make a few more rounds as Owen finishes his food and then tell them we have to leave.

"Why," Casey asks.

"Because we've had fun," I bark.

Over the dinner table, the boys are flooding Susan's ears with details of the day. She asks them if the rink was fun, and with sippy cups in their mouths, they're both giggling and nodding their heads.

"Oh my gosh, they loved it, Marc," she says. Casey is humming the hokey-pokey. "How did you know they'd love it this much?" she asks. "You're so good with them. How did you find out about this place? Was it great?" I told her it was, but didn't have the heart to ruin it by going on to say what a bad sport I'd been.

"Dad was pushing me on the trike so, so fast," Casey says. "And we were passing all the kids."

"Me too!" says Owen.

"And he was lifting us way up in the air like we were flying," Casey says.

"And *Coke* too!" Owen yelps.

"Daddy gave you *Cokes?*" Susan asks with a mock of outrage. The boys thrill. "Well, all I can say is you're lucky your dad took you there."

The boys continue on about the day and it's all good — only good. I listen silently and realize that their brilliance lies in the fact that I could have waltzed them into the rink with antlers strapped to their foreheads and it would have been fine — different from the rest but it's just how we do it — no problem. It was a day with their father and they'd have it no other way.

As they go on to give Susan all the long details, I'm struck by the essential peace they have with themselves. And I wonder when it was that I lost mine — lost the knowledge that with all things, there is no better passage to embrace than your own — that when you measure yourself against anyone else's yardstick, you always come up short. Casey and Owen pay no attention to the majority or minority, who is with a father, who is with a nanny, who is with a grandmother. There is no consideration of how they should be or what they should have — no looking outside of themselves to define what is inside. Every fiber of their existence is blindly self-accepting. They shout it from the rooftop during every waking second of every minute — *This is us. This is our life. It's not better or worse, or too much this or too little of the other — it's just our life. So let's make the most of it. We're burning daylight.*

Let's do something.

The first spring in the country after moving from New York, I plucked a bleeding heart flower and took it apart in front of the boys, knowing that each piece was supposed to be something. I remember, when I was a child, my mother turning the pieces into beautiful little charms that told a fantastic story. Of course, she did it as only a mother could. Of course, I'll never be a mother. But I gave it a try.

"Here are the mugs," I said to the boys as I peeled apart the outer sepals. "For your coffee — drink up, boys." They did. "Then come the fishhooks," I said, separating the corolla. We baited them with minnows and caught huge walleyes. "Next come the shovels, so we can bury the bones." They took the stamens carefully and pantomimed digging. "And finally," I said holding the pistil, "the whisky bottle — throw it over your shoulder and shout, *Yeehaa.*"

Susan smiled when she came home that night as the boys showed her what their father had taught them. She waited until they were in bed to tell me how she remembered doing it. I realized only as she carefully pulled the flower apart and identified each piece, that there is a mother's bleeding heart, and there is a father's bleeding heart, and that one is not better than the other unless you make it so. The pieces lying in a line across the kitchen table between us were only as different as the side of the room you happened to see them from. A father's mugs are a mother's swans, a father's fishhooks are a mother's fairy slippers, his shovels are her earrings, and the bottle — a father's is for whisky and a mother's is for perfume.

"Or champagne," Susan said very seriously as she tried to remember. Then she smiled. "Some of us girls made the bottle for champagne."

THE RABBIT

Three days before I was to give the keynote speech for a statewide conference in Virginia on children at risk, two boys in Littleton, Colorado, committed an atrocity that, even on the day it happened, felt historic. After four and a half years as a child abuse investigator, I'd been asked to articulate the silver lining around a good many dark clouds. This particular incident, however, put me at a loss for words.

"We'd like you to say something about the Colorado tragedy," one of the conference organizers told me the night before my speech. I agreed that something needed to be said but was hopeful that two boys planting thirty bombs in their school and unleashing semiautomatic weapons on their classmates was an aberration, and it's always wrong to draw sweeping conclusions based on an aberration. Who can say, exactly, what forces conspire in a childhood to create such an outcome? The most anyone can ever give it is their best guess, and the rest is just hoping for the sun to shine again, which it always does. From the moment it happened, the talking heads were out in force, trying to make sense of it all, and you got the feeling that despite their displays of conviction, most of them from the President on down had their fingers crossed under the table.

When I was growing up, there were no such things as school shootings, but there was still brutality, cruelty. Not on the level of a school shooting but the same at heart — different only in magnitude when compared with some of the things I watched my friends do. As I recall, kids were usually aware of the strange ones — *he's one of those,* you'd say — and everyone knew you had seen him impale a live mouse with an eightpenny nail on an otherwise normal sleepover. Aware as we were of these kids who crossed the line, few of us were completely innocent or totally immune to the seduction of cruelty.

There was a neighborhood club of nine- and ten-year-olds where I grew up that had a very coveted membership. Once in, you could enter all the secret forts that were scattered through the fields and forests, under pine trees and old stream hollows, way up in the treetops — some no more than a few boards nailed together with a knotted rope leading up to them. There was a secret handshake, a primitive but effective secret language; there were competency requirements, mostly having to do with how good you were with a pellet gun and how fast you could hop rocks up the river. You had to be able to sprint barefoot down a gravel road. You had to race through the forest without hitting a tree. You had to be able to catch a snake with your hand — sneak up on it and snatch it just behind the head without getting bitten. I remember a kid with a lot to prove, grabbing a large snake just a little too far back from the head. It rolled itself around like a fat brown whip and slapped its flimsy mouth around the fleshy part of the kid's palm just below his thumb. Instead of screaming and shaking it loose like any normal kid, he just looked up at us with a small, unconvincing smile and chirped, "Doesn't hurt. Doesn't hurt." We watched in horror as the snake coiled around his forearm and slowly pushed its head deeper into his hand. After about thirty seconds, the kid began to turn green around the edges. He smiled weakly, looked down at the snake one more time, and then broke into a total meltdown, hollering, galloping in circles, and flailing his hand through the air as if it were on fire. He ran home in tears and we didn't see him for several weeks.

Like any club, ours had an initiation. This one was simple — three things. First, you had to put a bug in your mouth. Any old bug. This wasn't as bad as it sounds, because you got to choose your bug. Smarter kids would select something along the lines of a small, crisp ant to hold between their tongue and palate until club members finished a slow five count. The kid with a lot to prove chose a grasshopper. He didn't last the count.

After the bug, you had to swing naked across the river on an old jute rope that looked like it was hung there by pioneers. Over time, jute turns to thistle and the toughest thing here wasn't the hoots and jeers of the others, but wrapping your legs around the rope and lowering your bare butt against the knot.

Finally, there was one last thing. You had to catch a minnow, hold it by the tail, bring it in close to your face, and watch it until it died. We called this "throwing a floater" because after the fish was dead and you threw it back to the river, that's just what it did. This part of the initiation was carried out in a less formal way than the first two. You were allowed into the club after swinging across the river, but it was understood that at some point, you'd have to complete this last requirement. We'd be down by the river and it was — *hey, did Pete throw a floater yet?* And then, sad-looking Pete and much-sadder-looking small fish, there together with Pete, proving to the rest of us that along with being fast and brave and funny, he could also be cruel. The scene was repeated every spring — would-be members of the club, standing along the edges of the riverbank in a solemn staredown with a small, flickering fish. Call it boys being boys, call it exploring the bounds of the forbidden or children trying to exert control into an uncontrollable world, call it transference or modeling or scapegoating or any other thing. Cruelty by any other name is still the same. It's with us at the start and with us to the finish. I see it in my boys and I see it in myself. The only difference between the sinners and the saints is what they end up doing with it.

———

Fading lilac and emerging wisteria play their fragrant symphony through the breeze of this late spring morning. Casey and Owen dart up the lawn, their arms floating and bouncing above their heads like conductors of an orchestra on the run. Duke races behind them, his brindled coat flickering under the filtered light of a low canopy of walnut branches. He was a purebred a few months back, but now his dark brown winter hair has given way to dull red patches, courtesy of great-granddad Brittany on his father's side.

The boys let the chickens out of the coop. The Sebrights are always first to emerge, the golds and then the silvers — hawklike, their black-rimmed feathers close to their bodies, their eyes bright and searching. The Arucanas follow, frantically darting their mismatched heads in every direction, their feathers like fluffed-up theater wigs. Then come two no-nonsense partridge rocks that the boys and I hatched from eggs, and, finally, eleven young chicks that wandered in from the woods one day and decided to stay. I top off the hoppers with feed and fill the waterer by the stream while the boys scatter handfuls of grain along the ground. The birds peck madly at the corn pieces, leaving the oats and barley like untouched chocolate liqueurs in a Whitman Sampler.

C. R. gets a handful and a scratch behind the ears. Duke gets a handful. The quail get a little. Then comes the rabbit.

"C'mon, boys," I shout. "Let's do the rabbit." Only for me, "doing" the rabbit is feeding him; for the boys, "doing" the rabbit is *doing* the rabbit. They bring sticks. The chickens are too fast, the dog too lovable, the cat has claws, but woe to the rabbit, as if almost designed by nature to be abused by children — the expressive range of a trout and so much easier to get ahold of. The boys reach the door of the small barn that holds his hutch. We call it the Mermaid House. Evil grins forecast their intentions.

"No sticks, guys," I say as we stand on the step up to the barn. They don't move. "Owen: put down the stick. Casey: put down the stick."

Before having them, one of the biggest misconceptions I had about living with children was that as long as I made sure always to be on the side of fairness, I wouldn't have to argue and negotiate. I wouldn't have to debate with them about whether or not they should run with a pencil in their mouth if I could get them to understand the consequences of falling. The skill in parenting, I thought, wasn't about setting limits as much as it was about being on the right side of things. I wouldn't have to oppress my children's desires, because if I showed them the good path, and it was actually a good path, they'd take it.

Wrong. Unless there's a strong argument for beating a caged rabbit that I haven't heard of.

"We're not gonna hit him," Casey says unconvincingly. Owen is still grinning. "We're just holding them. We just wanna hold these sticks — right, Owen?" Owen's grin widens. "Owen says we're just gonna hold them, Daddy, and not hit the rabbit — just hold them, that's all."

"Why do you want to just hold them?"

"Just — just — just . . ."

"Just what?"

"Just so we can just . . . just . . ." He doesn't have an answer.

"No hitting?"

"Sure, okay, Daddy," he fires. Owen nods. Like a fool, I let them in with the sticks. They hover like angels for exactly eight seconds before chucking the wings and charging the rabbit. I grab them by the backs of their shirts just as they make contact. The rabbit slips around behind me and thumps the floorboard.

"Hey, listen," I say, the boys dangling from their shirts on either side of me — smiling because no matter what I say, they've already won. "Drop the sticks." They do. "Now, is that nice? Is hitting with a stick a nice thing?" But it's so hard not to be a hypocrite — is holding your children by their shirts a nice thing?

I set them down.

"Guys, this is the rabbit's house," I begin — a door I've painted a hundred times. They look up at me, their eyes so quiet and listening I can almost believe that this time, the paint might stick. I've tried threats, distractions, bargains, but never an appeal to their good common sense. "We're in the rabbit's house, we have to be nice to the rabbit in his house. This is the place where he feels safe. You know, like when you run into your room and duck under the covers? Right? That's where you go to feel safe. Everyone needs a place to go that feels safe — even rabbits."

I walk to the corner of the barn by a stained-glass window and sit down on an old chair. The boys are standing together in the middle of a mound of hay, their heads down, their faces guilty, a Norman Rockwell tableau — *The Cruel Little Boys* — long sticks at their feet, the rabbit in the far corner behind them looking on in anger.

"Do you like this rabbit?" I ask. They both nod. "If you like something, do you try to hurt it? . . . If someone likes you, do they hit you? . . ." They shake their heads. "How do you think it feels to be hit with a stick? Do you think it hurts?" Casey nods. "Do you want to hurt the rabbit?"

"I don't want to hurt him," Casey says.

"If you hit him with a stick, you'll hurt him."

"I don't want to hurt him," he says again.

"Then don't hit him."

"I won't hit him."

"Owen."

"Okay, Daddy," he says, his face held loose to keep from smiling.

"Don't hit the rabbit."

"I not hit him, Daddy."

They turn and creep up to the rabbit, needling into the hay on either side of him. His ears pop up. They carefully run their small hands over his face and back. The ears spring upright after each pass of their hands — his upbringing in a third-grade classroom has made him quick to forgive.

I watch closely from my chair because unless this is some kind of breakthrough morning, I know what's coming next. Everyone waxes romantic about kids and animals. *How nice for the children,* people usually say when they see our setup. I give the predictable warm smile and nod, wondering as I'm doing so, what they'd say if I told them that all the boys really want to do with our animals is see what happens when you throw a rock at them. They fool you at a visit to the local petting zoo with their kind looks and soft curious touch. If left unsupervised, most children just want to see how fast an animal can run.

After an unprecedented minute of kindness, Casey and Owen are still petting softly. I'm about to believe that this could be the morning we've turned the corner. Yellow and blue light streams down and cradles around them from the stained-glass window on their end — very much the romantic version of children and animals. They take turns running their hands from nose to cottontail. I refrain from going gaga with *positive reinforcement* so that they might understand the simple joy of an animal on their own without me narrating it into their foreheads.

Casey begins to pat the bunny. He's read the book. "Pat the bunny, Owen," he says, and Owen does. They laugh. Owen's read the book too. "Pat bunny," says Owen, and Casey does. But then the third pat is more like a hit. They laugh. Owen stands and gives a little kick.

"*BOYS!*" I shout, a little louder than I mean to. The three of them crouch. I follow with a stare that they understand, and they're back to petting. There are occasional good mornings where everyone behaves, but just as many go like this no matter what tack I take. We bring carrots and they become arrows, lettuce becomes the blindfold, and then the fun begins. The soft, adoring gaze turns sour. The light stroke on the head deteriorates. One of them will shout to make the rabbit snort. Then kick to make it thump. Then spook to make it jump. No matter what I do. I'm able to spare the rabbit from the worst of it but walk out of the barn with my nerves shot because I can't believe that in this soft, golden light with an animal so helpless, I have to beg my boys for a kindness as small as their touch.

But I should know better because I've been there.

A little older, in my own golden light along the banks of the river behind my house in Wisconsin, trying to throw a floater, no one was there to tell me to be kind, and I wasn't.

In the beginning of the summer, after I'd done the bug and the rope swing, I told my friends in the club that I was a full-fledged member because, on my own, I'd also done the minnow. Since I fully intended to, it didn't feel like a lie to say that I had. The fact that I actually hadn't started to gnaw on me by the middle of the summer, and so one very early, cool morning, I decided to go to the river and get it done.

It wouldn't be the first time I had killed an animal. When you grow up in the country, sooner or later you find yourself in a position where you have to kill something or watch it suffer. There wasn't a month that went by without some half-broken animal hobbling into the yard to see how much blood it could spread across the dandelions before convulsing and then lying still — eyes glittering dark and watery at the edges, head cocked into the ground as if intensely interested in something hiding under a blade of grass. I had killed before, but there had always been a good reason for it, something that took the sting out of the act. I did it fast and I didn't watch. I put the barrel in the right place and pulled the trigger. If I was caught without my .22, I used a rock for the kindness. But killing for killing's sake — killing just to bring the whole thing right up to your face and watch its slow progression would be a whole different thing.

I walked up to a small tributary that roiled with fish every spring. There were plenty of them in the Little Eau Pleine River — pickerel, shiner, striper, chub, cat, sucker — no trout, no bass — sticker fish, sunnies, yellow bellies, blackies, whities, carp even, fish good for bending a pole but not so hot for the frying pan. There were turtles and crawdads, mussels, frogs, leaches, snails, but mostly fish, and where there are fish, there are minnows. There were a lot of minnows. A deep spot in the stream just before it ran into the main river was black with them. I knelt down in the moss lining the hole and lowered both arms into the water. With my face just inches from the shimmering surface, I rolled my hands through the dark pool. Each pass of my arms made fish bloom on the top of the water and then rush back down to face the current. With my arms still, the pool felt like it ran with electric current, fish criss-crossing over my palms and through my fingers, nipping my elbows like static shocks.

Slowly, I flexed my hands within the mass until closing in on a single fish — a sticker fish, we used to call them because of the row of spines along the back that could draw blood if you caught them just so. Carefully, I pinched its tail between my thumb and forefinger, and raised it up to my face. Its mouth jawed the air easily at first, but soon the flex of its gills grew desperate. I steeled my eyes to keep from looking away. The body twitched and then slowly bent upward. I felt a squeeze in my chest as each gasp grew longer. The mouth stretched wide and popped spasmodically. I clenched my lips, drew it in closer to my face; thirty more seconds passed like thirty days, and then I flung it back into the water, where it turned to its side for a moment and then shot like a dart into the dark mass of its brothers. Alive.

I made several attempts that morning, a few more that summer and then the summer after that, but every fish I tossed back into the river swam away. I could never throw a floater.

"*Casey,*" I say, just as he's about to push the tip of his stick into the rabbit's eye. I'm too overwhelmed by his lack of empathy to even react. The rabbit is unblinking even though the point of the stick is no more than an inch away. "What are you trying to do there?" I ask.

"Poke the rabbit's eye," he says matter-of-factly, as if he can't imagine what could be wrong with it. I sink into the chair feeling defeated after all the miles I've driven with them toward kindness only to find that I've just barely begun.

"Why?" I ask.

"Because I just want to," he says coldly. He can sense my bewilderment. He puts the stick down and lets out an impatient breath. I lean down to him from my chair.

"But *why,* Casey?" I ask, almost in a whisper. He shakes his head like I'd never understand.

"*Because I just wanted to, I told you,*" he hisses.

And he could be right about that. Even though I've been there, I'm couched by the sudden fear that my boys could grow up to do something terrible — that kindness in them would wither away if I didn't water it every day — that the young boys all over the country who keep popping up in the headlines were once just toddlers with parents who grew tired of begging them to be kind. Mischief with a rabbit may seem small when held up against a backdrop of the world's evils, but all seeds are small when compared to their matured growth.

The only difference between this morning and all the other mornings that I've had to peel them off the rabbit is that I finally realize that their affinity for cruelty is here to stay. I'm not so sure I can ever do anything more than to teach them how to wrangle it, how to keep it from running them over.

The boys pick up their sticks as we leave the rabbit, rushing out the door and down the lawn with them high above their heads, poking at the sky. I close the door behind me and watch them until they're almost to the house. They seem small, cradled between the curve of the ground and the wide-open sky, but the sticks are still large, looming above their heads like dark scepters. The boys exchange words that I can't hear and then crash the sticks together in the air. The weight of them throws their small bodies off balance as they swirl awkwardly at one another. Each slow swing takes their entire effort to muster. I resist the urge to intervene in hopes that they might work things out to a reasonable conclusion on their own.

The sticks crash together again, Owen maintains the momentum of his swing through a full circle and brings the stick around into Casey's side. Casey starts to cry. He swings back in anger and catches Owen across the shoulder. Owen cries. A one-all score. And they both just stand there crying at each other, unable to grasp the full story of what has happened, each of them understanding only that he's been hit, not that he's also been hitting. The sticks sway ominously above their heads, ready for more — a stick is always ready for more, although it looks like the battle is over for now.

Suddenly, what they're holding aren't sticks anymore but materialized objects of the burden that each of them will carry through the rest of their lives. The sticks can be laid aside in the grass, but the spirit of those sticks will always be with them. As they slowly trudge up to me in tears, I can see how ridiculous I've been to think that I could teach them kindness with a few short discussions in a rabbit house — that kindness is a place they would arrive at, putting meanness and cruelty behind them like diapers and baby clothes.

It's taken the constant lesson of their example for me to finally understand that the road to kindness is a journey that takes a lifetime, and that as we strive to get there, we carry our sticks along the entire distance. If two young children, unblemished by life's hardships, well fed, well cared for, stimulated, loved, coddled, mentored, on a perfect morning in the perfect setting can fall so easily to the draw of cruelty, how much easier is it for autonomous, competitive, self-obsessed, self-serving, overworked, stressed-out adults — especially when we no longer have the parent on our shoulder to tell us when we're slipping. Until this morning, I would have never imagined that the one thing keeping us on the perimeter of paradise could be something so plain and so simple as a stick.

If it were something they had meant to teach me, the boys would be smiling this morning because I finally just got it — simple kindness as a means to no other end than itself is not something that springs up and flourishes on its own. Compassion is cultivated. Empathy needs watching over. It's not enough to simply plant the seeds. Their fruits are not native to the soul. Left to itself, the untended heart grows cold.

The fact is that it's just too easy to be cruel, it's a jacket that fits too well, a silk hat we slip on and then forget we're wearing. The boys will have to learn to appreciate the benefits that come from being kind. What I have to remember for myself is that anything that's been learned has to be recalled, anything recalled must be studied, and anything studied must be drilled. So above all, kindness is a drill — one that never ends because no matter how well we think we have it down, somewhere deep inside, each one of us carries a stick.

Back in Virginia, I'm staring out into a sea of faces. Expectations are high — according to the programs in the lobby, I'm an expert in my field. But my idea of an expert is a person who is never without an answer, and that answer is always very good and very accurate. I'm hard pressed to find something very good and very accurate to say about the Littleton tragedy. From my hotel room, I watched the news right up to the point where I had to leave to give the speech. The experts on every channel were searching desperately for something very good and very accurate to say. No one was really coming up with anything. It didn't stop them from talking incessantly, however. To say, *who really knows what it means, who can actually say why it happens,* doesn't make for very good television. It doesn't make for very good speeches either. Even if it's the truth.

"I've been asked to say something about what happened in Littleton, Colorado," I began after a brief introduction. People in the front rows leaned forward a bit, unaware of the common mistake of expecting a writer who sits with his thoughts for hours before putting them to paper to say something very good and very accurate off the cuff. With a last-second stroke of luck, I had glanced through the lead editorial of the morning's *New York Times* and found a train of thought to launch me in the right direction.

"As we look to find a motive for what happened, even if only for selfish reasons — so that we can quarantine these tragic events, keeping them a safe distance from our everyday lives — it will be easy to place blame for what happened on a myriad of outside sources: guns, Hollywood, the Internet, music. There will be strong arguments put forth for the control of these and other outside influences in order to avoid another disaster like this one — arguments for a number of measures that will amount to no more than quick fixes. In the end, it's not what we keep our children from that will save them. It is what we put into them in the first place. The effort to keep them flying straight and true is one that should last their entire lifetime."

As I looked out across the gathering, it seemed as though this note struck a chord. I continued in this vein, stopping just short of the complexity that works so well in conversation but is disastrous during an off-the-cuff moment in a speech. The crowd seemed satisfied, the conference planners smiled and nodded. I took a drink of water and set the glass next to my left hand, resting on the stack of papers that was the speech I was about to deliver.

Fingers crossed.

THE OLD MAN

PART THREE

I've always envied people who have a real connection to country music. Those with uncles who played mandolins on the porch and talked about things like mad dogs or moonshine or powder burns. Folks who could make fried chicken. I had a friend who liked country music because it reminded her of her "daddy." She called him that without a hint of anything false about it. I never heard my dad say anything up or down about Hank or George or Tammy. I get Del McCoury and his brothers shaking the walls of the barn just the same, Buddy Miller and his wife, Julie, for foot stomping, Steve Earl and old Merle, Willie and Loretta and Iris Dement, but no matter how loud I play them, the plain fact is that my love for their music has no roots. It sprang up like ivy and has grown without tending.

The first instrument I learned to play was a grand piano,

one of those huge, shining black ones that lie beached across your better living rooms and concert halls and the only musical device with the distinction of being sold in furniture stores. If the first harmonicas had been wrapped in cabinetry you could set a martini glass on, there would have been a lot more parents making sure their children picked it up in grade school recital. The first song I learned to play had been passed from my grandmother to my father, who passed it on to me and my younger brothers: the "St. Louie Blues." My immediate family on both sides came out of a small, snow-covered border town in northern Maine. As far as I know, none of them have ever set foot in St. Louis. But what I've come to know about heritage is that if you're not given one, you steal one. And I've had to steal most all of mine as I've gone along.

My dad's father died when he was just ten years old. Dad was the youngest child in a family that was mostly grown. He told me he remembers waking one morning to a commotion of relatives milling about the house in their best clothes. He wandered into his parent's room to find his father situated neatly on his bed, dead. He told me he was overcome with a sudden feeling of guilt because he'd stepped into a place where children didn't belong — seen his father in a way that would have made him angry. He left the room quickly, knowing something was wrong but not finding out until much later in the day that his father had passed away. No one had told him. Which was very much in keeping with his whole childhood, as far as I can tell.

One day, he got a shotgun, a 12-gauge Remington pump

that he'd picked out of a Sears catalog because it looked nice in the picture. His mother bought it for him when he'd hit an age that meant he was old enough to be sent into a field by himself with the gun and a box of shells to see what would happen when you put the parts together and set them loose. At the time, that age was eleven. He knew the gun would buck like a green-broke mare, so he thought to hold the butt a few inches from his shoulder for the first shot — sort of a handgun stance with a shotgun. A very bad idea. He pulled the trigger and the gun slammed into him so hard that he put it in his closet and never fired it again.

The experience that afternoon would have been quite different had his father still been with him. I can only imagine how different. I can only imagine the way that difference might have filtered down to me. Dad told me on more than one occasion while I was growing up that he didn't precisely know how to be a father because, in a way, he never had one. And without a father, very little was passed to him in the way of heritage, so he in turn had very little to pass on to me along the lines of the son-this-is-the-way-we've-always-done-it kind of thing by the fireplace with a moose head on the wall and a cognac in his hand. But you can steal your heritage or you buy it out of the Sears catalogue and call it your own. The gun Dad shot one time, alone in a field — the one nobody told him to buy or showed him how to fire, is in my house. It looks as though it was passed down through generations of bear hunters. If you're not given one, your heritage becomes that you take what is not yours. My dad stole his shotgun and gave it to me. I stole my country music roots, and I'll give them to the boys, if they'll take them. It's just the way we've always done it.

This morning, they'll take them. The music is up high, and the three of us are slapping our boots against a new wood floor in a corner of the barn. The boards thump loudly underfoot to singers who croon about smoky mountains and backwater towns I can only imagine. Owen easily tricks Casey and me out of any self-consciousness, getting us both to move like two-year-olds. I try not to think about what a fool I must look like as I push my arms and legs to remember a time before dance moves.

Owen runs a few feet and then freezes with his legs spread apart. His trick, he calls it. *Daddy, look — a trick*. He runs and stops, his legs spread not quite as wide as his grin. He runs again, stops, bends his knees, throws his left arm out to the side and holds it.

"*Good trick*, Owen," I say — every aspect of life, no more than a dance — every dance, no more than a series of tricks done to music.

Casey bounces on his knees but stops and rolls his eyes as soon as I get a look at him. Then the three of us hold hands and hop in a circle. Soon I'm just the maypole, the boys satisfied only as long as I can swing them in a circle. I bring them round and round; the floorboards muddle beneath them as they look up at me, their chins pressed into my forearms, their faces spraying joy. The fiddles wheel through pentatonic major, the pedal steel weeps along the same line, the singers howl, my arms are burning — the boys shouting for

more, I lift my head and let my eyes go blurry against the
racing vertical strips of light that pour through the barn
walls.

It's not exactly possible within the definition of the word,
but it seems in this moment that the boys are passing a heritage on to me — this time, this feeling, these tricks — all of
it impossible if not for them. If a heritage is something that
defines those who receive it, if it sinks into your soul, going
far beyond traditions and possessions and entitlements into
the essence of where you're from and what you're made of,
then this is heritage. It doesn't matter who was born to whom.
I'm not the one begging them to swing from my arms every
time George Jones sings a drinking song.

After tuna sandwiches, several block towers, two *Curious
George* stories and the last half of a *Sesame Street* video, Casey
is still humming the music from our barn dance as I load
him and his brother into the stroller. We're off to see
Dick — our afternoons with the old man as much a stolen
heritage as any country music twang. Thousands of miles
away, the boys have grandfathers on either side of the family, but at their age, the one who dispenses the most candy
wins. Here, Dick has the real McCoys beaten hands down.

The stroller creaks under the weight as I hoist them inside. They grumble about for position, their round arms and
long legs poking awkwardly into the places that once fitted
them so neatly. I negotiate Casey into the back with the
promise that he'll ride the helm on the way home. Owen sits
forward, his torso hanging over the front bar that once cradled his chin. Casey's legs squeeze in around him, his knees
protruding sideways like the armrests on a captain's chair.

They look just this side of ridiculous, the way they're stuffed inside, but wouldn't have it any other way. They love to ride. Casey would ride in the backpack I carried him in as a toddler if there was any possible way of fitting him into it. Owen would ride to the doctor for a battery of shots if I took him there on my shoulders. It doesn't matter how it comes or where it's going, and if cramming into a small stroller with an unruly brother is the only way to pull it off, well then, they're all for it.

Most children know without ever being told that the time to ride is fleeting. As the oldest child, I discovered it almost immediately and watched with earthbound feet through a sour lens as the little ones were thrown endlessly around me. The realization took a little longer to arrive for my younger sisters but was no less painful when it did. When my time was up, I remember squeezing the last few rides out of my dad, pretending to be asleep while he carried me from the car to my bed. If it's not the single universal connection between people of all ages on every part of the planet, the love to ride has to be right up in the top five. I'm six one and 190 pounds, and if there were someone twice my size who could run full speed with me hugging their shoulders, I'd be all over it.

On the road, the suspicion index has risen considerably among passing cars as I push my swaying, overburdened load off to the shoulder when they pass. What I really need is one of those sleek new joggers on bicycle wheels with disk brakes and room for seven under the pull-down hood, but I have a faithful streak and can't bring myself to part with the gypsy wagon that has seen us through almost everything.

The wheels, once knobby and bright, ready to tackle the meanest streets New York City had to offer, have been worn smooth by their years of service. Despite repeated washings, the cloth hood and seat are mottled by a five-year steady drip of milk and orange juice. Graham cracker crumbs have become as significant a part of its workings as the grease in the wheels. Iron nails, ground down and bent over, have replaced rivets in the frame long since broken. The seat belt, like a web we diligently wrapped around Casey's shoulders and small torso for protection against the world, has been ripped out and lost. It's not the glossy beast it once was, but it still rolls like a dream, holds a four- and a two-year-old at the same time, and eats potholes like a bag of chips.

Two minutes on the road and the boys are sweating under their caps. It's not even noon, and the heat of the day is already playing its half-strung guitar. We haven't seen a steady rain in the last month and a half. My footsteps are heavy on the hot tar. Trees on either side of us are exhausted with sunshine. Their leaves cast a silvery sheen in the menacing brightness, many of them yellow and drifting from their branches into the still air. Through the haze, the hills loom like giant gray tidal waves of a surrounding earthocean that could suddenly advance with amazing speed and engulf the entire valley. I'm too pragmatic to say they seem restless and full of danger, even when they are, even when I know it's true.

In the still brilliance of this bright, shining late morning, I feel the same vague uneasiness as these hills. When I got out of bed a few hours earlier, I felt as if I could kick the walls out of the house for no reason at all. It's the feeling that creeps up on you without warning and without cause. Everything you eat tastes like fish, and your best shirt feels like a stranger and your boots do too. You find a problem in every conversation, and the Advil bottle goes down a little quicker than it used to. It's the lash in your eye and the kernel in your tooth and a knock in the engine and a hole in the bottle, a page ripped out and a dog on the loose and you can't find the keys — the gut ache that's not quite there and won't go away and *every damn thing is just so wonderful around here, we're all fine, I'm great, no problem at all — a little leak in the fuel line that we can't seem to locate but it should be just fine . . .*

I'd be more comfortable dragging these bags of sand if there was actually something wrong. When Susan gets this way, she doesn't have to worry that she's losing her mind. She takes a Midol and goes to bed early, waking up the next morning feeling fine and writing the whole thing off to hormones, the perfectly legitimate explanation for every unexplainable funk. What I'm feeling right now is less easily classified. I'm not so sure that it could ever be explained, but I know I'm going to a place where there will be answers. The boys always ask for Dick when the time is ripe for a harvest.

"Is Dick gonna have a little something for me, Daddy?" Casey asks as I turn the stroller off the road and down the long drive to the house where he works.

"Well, he might and he might not," I say.

"But maybe he has a candy for me and for Owen?"

"It's possible."

"And when we get there, he's gonna give it to us?"

"I don't know what Dick's got today," I say. "We're just stopping to say hello."

"Well, I'm gonna ask him to check and see if he's got a little something for me and for Owen."

"Listen, Case, I don't want you to ask Dick for candy the second you see him. Okay?"

"Why?"

"Because first you say, 'Hello!' when you see someone. Then you say, 'How ya doing?' And they say, 'Pretty good.' And then you talk a little bit — you tell them a little something."

"And then you can ask them for candy?"

"Well, okay. But you can't just walk up to them and ask for candy the first thing. Okay, Casey? I don't want you to do that."

"Why?"

"Because it's not polite. It's just not the way you do things." He turns forward in the stroller. "Casey?"

"Okay, Daddy," he says.

"We'll say hello first and not just ask for candy . . . Case?"

"Okay, Daddy."

We round the end of the drive and spy Dick, who is high up a ladder on the side of the house. "Hey there, old-timer!" he cheers and then shakes his head. "Just working on these windows here like always. Sure, and by the time I finish the last one, the first one's gonna need me again! Good to see ya —"

"*Dick, have you got a little something for me?*" Casey shouts up immediately. Dick tosses his head back with a big laugh. *"Have you got a candy for me and for Owen?"*

"Well, let me see about that," he says and backs carefully down the ladder, walking over to the open trunk of the Pontiac. "Let me see if I . . . why sure, here they are — hey, boys, we're in luck," he says, rising with a small package of bright orange crackers held up to either side of his face.

The boys grab the bags eagerly and they're off. The old man beams at them, and as I watch him, I know there's so much more there for the taking than bags of orange crackers. If I could find a way to muster the same blunt initiative, I'd reach out and grab at it just like them. *Dick — have you got a little something for me?* He's watching them run up the lawn, the orange crackers glowing in their hands, his fingers running through the bristles of his holstered brush almost as if on their own.

"Those are some good little deputies all right," he says, his smile a bit quieter than before. *Dick — have you got a little something for me?* He glances over as if he almost heard me. *A little something in the back of the Pontiac I could use to get me right? I'm in a bad way sometimes for no damn reason — danced with angels all morning in the barn but walked out feeling like everything is finished before I can ever get my arms around it. It all goes so fast, but the days last forever and there's still not enough time — I can barely keep up and I'm restless just the same. Where are we going, Dick? — what's it all for anyway — and what good is it when it's balanced on a thread so thin it can break at a touch. Have you got a little something for me? What the hell is the use sometimes?*

Casey and Owen crouch around the edge of a small cement pond filled with lilies and silt-brown tadpoles. Dick and I walk over, talking through the basics of weather and geography as well as a story or two about area merchants and their latest misdeeds — the bank teller who gave him an extra hundred-dollar bill and didn't say thank you when he returned it, the gas station that uses 87 octane in the 92 pump, shrinking deli sandwiches, and the rising cost of a suspension overhaul. Deep rivers run through both of us, but we're speaking in a code of politeness that keeps us from getting our feet wet and safely outside of any emotional no-trespassing zones. Even though I try to soften it, I admire Casey's up-front way of letting people know exactly what he expects out of an encounter. What he lacks in tact he makes up for with his honesty. *Have you got a little something, Dick?* Sometimes I have a feeling the old man and I could get through the deepest mysteries in the universe if we only knew how to break from the code.

The boys drop to their bellies. Their chins kiss the top of the water as they reach down through rays of sunlight and algae for tadpoles swimming to the bottom. Dick watches them, his eyes sparkling. The affliction I'm harboring at the moment keeps me just outside of it. I used to see it in my mother's eyes when she got to feeling this way — when everything around you is going right except your insides and the only thing to do is clean the hell out of every rug and window in sight. I've been with my boys for years now, and there are still days when I can barely handle the overwhelm-ing depth of stillness that tags along with them. The total lack of distractions leaves you no other choice than to gaze long and hard into the unencumbered heart of all that really matters. It's not something you can see from a mountaintop or from a thousand miles out on a raging ocean, even though most everyone is telling us that these are the kinds of dramatic places where you find these deep truths. I think it could be as simple as your connection to the heartbeat of the earth being directly proportional to the number of jelly toast sandwiches you make in a typical week. I really do.

Owen's arms arc through the dark pool behind an awkward army of tadpoles. Casey is brushing the surface of the water with his fingertips to study the ripples. Dick is seated on a wooden bench, watching them and saying things like *"Oh my"* and *"I'll be"* at the appropriate times, and I realize that nothing in my former life could have prepared me for the onset of this stillness — so penetrating in this moment that I can hear my own breathing. I gaze up into the brightness of this solitude and it occurs to me that emotions flying up and down for no apparent reason are not necessarily the onset of anything clinical or hormonal but simply the result of being immersed in a place so quiet that you can actually feel the fluctuation. A schedule emptied of the everyday props of distraction — traffic, headlines, deadlines, proposals, appointments — and for the first time I'm able to hear the sand falling away from under the footings of everything I know and love — a string snapping in every second — every moment, each heartbeat, every sunset passing forever.

And Dick and the boys are a double team, rushing me from opposite ends of the court to deliver the same message: this ain't gonna play on forever. It's something everyone knows intellectually, and then on a deeper level when someone close dies and you wonder exactly where they slipped off to, but a visit with Dick after a day with Casey and Owen brings it right into my face. I'm never so old as when I look into the boys' eyes and never so young as when I'm looking into the old man's. With them here on either side of me, I have no choice but to feel as old and as young as I've ever felt at the same time — such a change from my days racing up and down the streets of Manhattan with fashionable friends, where we'd turn up the volume of distractions whether it was music or the news or our jobs, or just maniacal laughter to keep from hearing a heartbeat.

In the middle of Cherry Valley with two small children and an old man exchanging their unique brands of solitude over a pool of tadpoles, it's the crush of time I'm feeling because the air is finally clear enough to get a read on the sheer velocity of it. The bittersweet side of appreciating life's most precious moments is the unbearable awareness that those moments are passing. *Have you ever felt that, Dick? Have you got a little something for me?*

"You hear about the snakes, Marc?" Dick asks in a low voice, his eyes dark and conspiratorial. It's hard not to assign a double meaning to everything he says. I tell him I haven't. He nods his head slowly, "They're coming down from all over the mountain."

"No kidding?"

"This drought we're in. Sure. Rattlers. Copperheads. They're coming right down the mountain looking for water. I meant to tell you."

"Thanks, Dick."

"Oh, you betcha. Lookin' for water. Sure. They're getting mixed up into everything. Can you blame 'em? Corn should be up to here by now," he says, crossing his hand over his chest. "A real mess. What we need is a good hard storm. Neighbor by you found a couple in his field. Guy up over here scared up a big one. Sure. It's no good, I tell you. Fella your age would make out all right if he mixed up with one, but me or the boys there, if one got into us we'd be in some hot water. Sure."

"Sure."

"You bet."

Have you got a little something?

"You can never be too careful these days," he says. "Just about everything can turn into trouble. My gosh."

"Sure."

"Oh, you bet."

Anything at all? What do seventy plus years get you, Dick? Seventy years, combat in Korea, losing a daughter, a heart attack — what do you say after all that? Where does it get you in the end? Tell me there's more to all this than just getting older. Have you got a little something?

"A good hard storm would send those snakes back into the hills. That's what we really need around here. You bet. A good long storm would get things going right," he says, and if he thinks I'm crazy for the way I'm searching his face for meaning, he doesn't show it. "Any bears by you yet?" he asks.

"Just one across the driveway that kept on moving."

"Cubs?"

". . . No, Dick. No cubs."

"Well, stay in the house, by gosh, if you see the cubs with her."

"Right."

"There'll be more. Everything's coming down for water. The fields are as sick as I've seen them, Marc. Can't really remember ever seeing the corn like this. A good long drink of water is what we really need here."

We spend a little more time together. He brings me to a heavy old door with dimpled glass panes that he's just re-hung after stripping, recaulking, and repainting it. Then he brings me to a sash he's been sanding. He asks me isn't it smooth, and I say it is. We talk about the sheetrock shortage in the area, the building boom, and how much we like the old houses even though they're a constant chore. The boys finish their crackers and ask for more. Dick gives them an-other small bag even though I beg him not to because he's taken it straight out of his lunch box. I pack them up to go before they swindle him out of his sandwich and potato chips. We walk back along the road, Casey and Owen's mouths sweet with cookies and my mind swimming with the thought of a storm that could cure the fields and send the snakes and bears up the mountain.

Back where they belong.

The following week, I receive a call that Dick is under-going emergency surgery for the removal of his kidney. Tests on the organ will show whether or not the cancer has spread to the rest of his body.

I waited until a few days after the surgery before going to the hospital to see him. I hadn't called his family to ask how it all went or to see if he was receiving visitors. He had a wife whom I'd met only briefly. I'd seen two of his sons in passing. I didn't feel as though they would want to talk to me about something so personal as Dick's condition, especially if it wasn't good. I knew that if he was feeling well at all, he would want to see me, but I wasn't so sure that his family would know it. Driving to the hospital, I wondered if Dick had ever spoken to them about our friendship. Did they know that there was someone else who would want to see him pull through this? Or had I misread our relationship as something more than it was? Was there the smallest place for me to occupy in this very personal time? Standing at his bedside, would I be seen as a visitor or an invader? Before getting there, I picked up a large bag of peanut chews for Dick and a potted miniature rose bush for his wife. If I stepped into the room and sensed they didn't want me there, I could drop them off and go, no harm done.

The closer I got to the hospital, the more I began to worry about whether or not an unannounced visit was the smart thing to do. Would Dick be sour with the rigors of recovery? Would he be on heavy medications? Connected to machines? In pain? Sedated? I had always seen him in the perfect setting and had no idea how it would be to visit him without a background of dappled light and the sound of rustling leaves. Would he be uncomfortable in my presence the way some men are about being caught with their boots off? By the time I reached the floor, I had half a mind to leave the candy and flowers at the nursing station with a get-well-soon note.

The door to his room was open. I stood in the entryway and looked inside. His wife was seated in a chair at the foot of his bed. Dick was concealed behind a half-drawn curtain. As I walked into the room, his wife looked up, startled. I set the candy and flowers on a desk by the wall. She stared at me with her eyebrows up and a curt smile that said, wrong room, sir.

"Dick?" I asked softly as I leaned in around the curtain.

"Well, I'll be," he said, reaching up with both hands to grasp mine, a smile exploding across his face. "I don't believe it — my gosh. It's Marc, from the valley," he said to his wife. "You remember Marc, sure. Thanks for coming." I glanced around the bed for the gurgling hospital hardware I was certain I'd find. There was nothing. Dick was up and moving without strings. His cheeks were bright red as though they'd seen a whole morning of raking the leaves on a fall day.

"I figured it would be pretty tough to get a peanut chew around here," I said. "I thought I'd bring you a supply to hide under the bed." He laughed generously, even though I could see it was painful for him. He held on to my hands just long enough for me to notice how different it felt from all the handshakes we'd exchanged in the past, long enough for me to understand that this grasp was all I was really there to do. There's nothing you can say to a person in a hospital bed that can be communicated by any better means than with two clasped hands.

"My gosh," he said, with a shake of his head. "Well, can you believe this? Look at me." He let go of my hands and lifted his gown to reveal what looked like a white sleeping bag wrapped around his middle. "Sure. And the doctor comes up to me after the surgery — young guy — he says, 'Dick, you probably don't feel like the luckiest man in this town today, but you are.'"

"They removed the kidney?"

"Took it clean out. Oh, you bet. Said it might have killed me in a month if they hadn't found out about it. Sure, and I was just coming in for a checkup. Can you imagine that? I tell you. It's a lucky thing. My gosh."

I glanced at his wife on the other side of the bed. She was looking at me with a small, polite smile and eyes that were scared as hell. I asked her if there was anything I could get her on the outside, if she needed anything done at the house. She thanked me and said her sons were taking care of it, and I suddenly knew that my need to help them far outweighed their need to be helped.

"Well, if there's anything at all," I said.

"Oh, you bet," Dick said, waving his hand. "Tell me, how are my little deputies?"

"They'd be right here with me if the hospital allowed it."

"Why, sure they would."

"Wanted to come see you."

"Did they?"

"They sure did."

"Oh boy."

"But the hospital wouldn't let me bring them. I called."

"Sure."

"Wanted to come, though. They're too young."

"Sure — they're too young. Well, you tell them as soon as I get out of here, I'll have a little something for them," he said with a wink and a laugh, and I knew he must have caught a glimpse of my face when Casey asked him for a treat this last time.

"I'm actually trying to get them to stop doing that."

"Oh hey, what's the harm?"

"Well, I guess." His wife asked if I had a picture and I pulled out my wallet to show her. She wanted to hear some of their latest pranks, so I told her a few. Dick lying in a bed with one of his organs removed so it wouldn't just sit there and kill him and we're talking about me. I put the wallet away and didn't feel like leaving just yet but didn't really have anything else to say. "Does it hurt?" I asked.

"Oh, you betcha," he said, still smiling. "Boy, something awful. Oh man. A little better today, though. I woke up this morning thinking about the work I needed to do on those windows — can you believe it? Sure. So I must be getting better if I'm lying here thinking about those windows. Boy, and I was just about to prime that glazing I put down, and now we're supposed to finally get that rain and I'm stuck in this place. I'll have to pull it out and start all over if that glazing gets wet before I can get it covered." His wife assured him one of their boys would take care of it, but I knew all he was really talking about was his desire to get back up on a high ladder.

"So what happens next here?" I asked as a delicate way to find out whether or not they knew if the cancer had spread.

"Well, . . . another night or two, they think, and I should be able to go home," he said, his hand held up with fingers crossed.

"And then you'll be all right," I said. The smile drifted

from his face, and his eyes got clear like when I asked about the wallet picture of his daughter. I was back in the place where tragedy obliterates all bubbly conversation and accompanying animated gestures. Back in the place where there is only truth.

"Well, not necessarily," he said slowly, "not necessarily." His wife looked to the window. Dick and I stared across each other's shoulders. Then his lips bent into a small, ironic smile. "Boy, the only thing you can ever really lose in this life is time. Ain't that the truth? I don't care what anyone says. You never can get back time. Sure. . . . It's what I've been thinking about in this bed — you can never get back time. . . . They're doing tests on the kidney. Results should be in by tomorrow. We'll know for sure by then."

The first spots of rain began to appear on my windshield as I drove out of the hospital lot, the kind that dry on the glass almost as soon as they hit. A rain cloud with the courage and original thinking to break from the line of storms stretching from Chicago to Buffalo had come on a straight course through western Pennsylvania and headlong into the high-pressure system that had been bullying the eastern region for the past month and a half. A welcome giant on the horizon, the road like a dark cord winding straight into its swollen belly. Driving into it, I thought about my vague uneasiness and how good I have it if I can find it in me to suffer the pain of nothing wrong at all. In the face of a genuine crisis, mine is pure luxury — not desirable, not walnut trim on the dash, but a luxury all the same. Probably a waste of time as well. The old man has a little something for me — a sweet for the boys and the smallest taste of his darkest storm to knock my perspective back on the track.

The rain was falling like it finally meant it by the time I pulled up the driveway. I jumped from the truck and rushed for home the way the bears and snakes must be doing up the mountain. Back where they belong. As I ran up the walkway, I could hear the stream that runs behind the house raging. With the ground still hard from the drought, most of the water was rolling off before it could do the plants any good. The first storm doesn't quench the soil's dryness as much as prepare it to receive the downpours that follow. The next bout of rain is the one that penetrates the ground to refresh the deepest roots. The first one just leaves you in shock. Only later, when it begins to sink in, can you start to make sense of it. At first, it just rolls off.

When I got into the house, Casey and Owen were standing on the windowsills, watching the storm.

"They want to go play in it," Susan told me. "I said they couldn't because of the lightning, but we haven't seen any yet. What do you think?"

"Maybe if they stay on the patio."

"Dad says okay if you stay on the patio."

They cheered and began stripping down to their skins. Susan and I followed them and sat on the porch where we could keep an eye on the sky. The boys stood naked under the shower with heads up, eyes closed, and mouths open wide.

"So how is Dick?" Susan asked over the peal of rain.

"Well, he's still Dick," I said. "Still talking windows, you know? His canary in the coal mine — as long as he's talking windows. . . . He seems all right."

"That's good. So he'll be okay."

"Well, no, . . . he might not be. They don't know yet if he'll be okay." Casey's eyelids flickered under the raindrops. Owen's face was smooth and relaxed, the skin over his chest shining with water. I tried to freeze them in my mind even as they seemed to be vanishing before my eyes. With the rain swelling in volume, the small silvery rivers running down the lawn began to disappear, replaced by wide, shallow pools of water that sank deep into the soil.

"He told me something," I began. "Just before I left him." And I felt the transformation as the words passed over my lips; the kind of shift in ground that deepens your understanding of everything, like when you fall in love and suddenly every song you hear, every poem and painting makes perfect sense. "He said, the only thing you can ever really lose in this life, is time." Susan smiled. "You can always make more money or get more things, but time is the one thing you don't get back once you've spent it." I hadn't fully considered Dick's last words until saying them out loud to Susan. This time they sank in. "I always knew it, but I guess I thought that by Dick's age, I'd be satisfied somehow. Like I'd had enough.

"Because you think about someone dying in their twenties or in their thirties maybe, and everyone always says it's such a shame because their life was cut short — but I think about Dick — a man in his seventies, and how much he enjoys just being on top of a ladder, how much he has to love his wife and his kids — *every* life is cut short. I don't care how old you are when it's time to go. You think about all these perfect pieces of an ordinary life on the plainest day — when could it ever feel like a good time to give them all back? Like after you've cornered the smallest gorgeous piece of all of this, you're supposed to reasonably hand it over after seventy or eighty years? We're supposed to leave without kicking and screaming because we've been around as long as a small oak tree? Seventy years as opposed to thirty makes handing it over fair somehow? . . . No way. The wind blows through my shirt the same as Dick's and doesn't feel any better because I'm half his age. I don't believe there is a life that ends that isn't cut short."

As I went on, Susan listened quietly like so many who relish and suffer their partner's monologues and love, hate, or simply understand them better than anyone ever could because of it. With hardly a word, she's helped me sort through so much. I felt as if I'd cornered a piece of something by the time I was finished, but the rain fell and the boys splashed and the world kept turning, regardless.

The storm lasted just long enough to make a statement without causing any damage. The wind bent the trees back and forth, pruning every superfluous leaf and branch, leaving behind only the parts that mattered. Every other nonessential thing ripped away and thrown to the ground. The following early morning saw a few light sprinkles, enough to bring the colors of the forest into vibrant relief but nothing as convincing as from the night before. Just after breakfast, I got a call from the woman who owns the house that Dick takes care of. She had just gotten off the phone with his family at the hospital and wanted to let us know that the test results had come in. The preliminary indications were good. The cancer had not spread. Except for his recovery from the surgery, this particular ordeal was over. The cloud had passed, leaving all who were under it relatively intact. I had felt the coolness of its crossing even from my vantage on the periphery. And it didn't change me as much as bring me back to what I'd always known but had lost somewhere in the relentless glare of a succession of perfect sun-shining days: time is the one thing you can never get back once you've spent it. Moments that pass are gone forever. Falling as deeply in love with as many people, places, and things as you possibly can — that's the best revenge on the unjust brevity of this fragile life.

I walked out to the porch and told Susan that Dick would be okay. We sat with our relief for a moment. I told her I loved her. I said that I had it made with her and that she should remind me of the fact whenever I forgot it. And suddenly, her eyes knew something that no words would describe. And her hair, dark curls shining in the sun, and the boys pushing trucks across the lawn, the forest behind them still wet with rain, colors rich and blazing, and every tree whose moist dark trunk met the sunlight, smoking with dew —

This time I saw it.

THE CRIB

This uncluttered time is fading. I feel it slip away with every old thing set aside and every new thing taken on. It's not always the big things that mark a change — not the graduation ceremony or the wedding bells, not the champagne toast or popping balloons and flowing streamers. Sometimes the biggest change is marked by nothing more than the smallest melody that's suddenly forgotten, the favorite set of jeans outgrown, the round cheeks that flatten, the lock of hair that turns from blond to brown.

There is nothing I can think of that quite describes the feeling of your youngest child giving up his crib. When it was Casey's time to move on, it wasn't quite the same because we were making way for Owen. We moved him aside to make way for the future. We pointed to a round belly and tried to explain, though we could hardly grasp it ourselves, that something inside would soon need a place to stay. But

Owen's move only makes way for the past. With no baby brother or sister on the way, the vacated crib will hold only memories.

I had actually attempted to do this earlier. Owen's future bed was being stored in the barn. I wanted to make room for some equipment and completely underestimated the significance of making the switch. A salient warning: The husband who dismantles a crib before his wife is prepared to do so should fully expect to be injured. I hadn't actually gotten very far — just the mattress out and the bumpers undone. When Susan got home and I told her what I intended to do, I was met by what can only be described as blunt force. I returned the room to its original condition, stopping just short of rehanging the mobile and greasing the runners. Later that night, when I checked on the boys, the crib seemed to say — more than Owen's presence in it — there is a baby in this home. That's the piece Susan wasn't yet willing to part with.

So we ignored the manufacturer's warning printed on industrial-grade, nuclear-proof plastic and riveted to the box spring. The one that says you're supposed to "discontinue use when child is able to use top rail as balance beam." I think it's important for parents to choose at least one printed warning to ignore. This was ours. We kept a permanent pile of pillows and blankets as well as our fluffiest clothing atop an old futon along the side of the crib and watched for close to a year as Owen's dismount evolved from full-face plants and shoulder-roll flips to belly flops and, finally, simple flying leaps.

During the extension of this crib period, I've become quite comfortable with the idea of him inside it. Susan's hesitation to take it down has given me an appreciation of it in the room, and now it's me who wants to leave it up. I have a feeling it's somehow related to the fact that the final count of our family is yet to be resolved. Susan has begun to quiz me about this with some regularity, but she does so at odd times — her way of getting a gut answer from me without the long and reasoned discussion. The way it comes up tells me she's thinking about it even more than she lets on. I'll be shaving and, through the door, it's *Do you ever see us having another child?* Or in the middle of trying to decipher the latest phone bill, *So what would you say if I told you I was pregnant?* Baby clothes are so much easier to take care of in a way that doesn't make predictions about the future. Who doesn't have a box of onesies in the attic that only need a good bleaching to be put back into service? But a crib won't sit so easily in a box for no reason. A crib must be dealt with.

"I think Owen is ready," Susan says over breakfast before leaving for work.

"I think he's *been* ready."

"Well, I think I'm ready then," she says. "Take the crib down today if you feel like it."

"Owen — are you ready to sleep in a real bed?" I ask. He nods over his bowl of cereal, his mouth dripping milk. He takes another bite. "There's no ceremony in him for this — look." He's staring into his bowl, chewing slowly. "I don't even think he cares," I say and walk over to his little table, crouching down in front of him. "You want me to put the crib away, Owen?" He nods. Another bite. Chewing. "Are you sure? You're ready to sleep in a bed? No more crib?" A sip of orange juice. He nods again, smiling now at my astonishment over his casual attitude. Like I'm asking if he's sure he wants a refill of Rice Krispies.

"You're right, Marc," Susan says. "He's been ready. Go ahead and take it down."

"Maybe if we fed him a little less —"

"I'll put sheets on his new bed tonight."

"— Maybe he wouldn't grow up so damn fast. You know if there were any possible way —"

"I know — it's true. I know what you're gonna say."

"I wouldn't mind him staying exactly the way he is for about the next ten years."

"If there was only a way — I know. You're not the only one. I love two and a half."

"I feel like I just got used to the idea of a house full of babies, and now they've gone off and become children."

"Two and a half doesn't last near as long as it should."

"Well, . . ."

"What?"

"Nothing a little visit to the local mad scientist wouldn't take care of."

I tell Susan I'll get the crib down and tucked away while she's gone. Everyone signs off on the action, including Casey, who launches into Owen about the many virtues of a bed — a mattress surrounded not by wooden bars but by open air! Freedom! Control of your own destiny! More room for toys! Bouncier! Most significantly, Owen will be able to join him on his nightly pilgrimage to our room. This point is suspiciously omitted.

Within an hour of Susan's leaving, I'm up in the boys' room with the tools in my hands. This would have been so much easier on my first attempt. Before I had time to think about what it meant. Before recognizing that I'd become so comfortable with it in our lives. But if anything can universally be said about life with children, it's that they make no concessions to comfort. On every level, from a full night of sleep to a warm spot on the couch to an uninterrupted train of thought, Casey and Owen have hurled me from the security of the smallest routines, always forcing me to keep up with them as they move on to something new.

Standing at the head of the crib with the drill in my hand that will happily dismantle this time in my life, I'm thinking back to when we picked it out — Susan eight and a half months pregnant, a hot August day in the East Village of Manhattan, slogging through unair-conditioned isles of newborn equipment. It felt like we needed one of everything but we could barely afford the breast pump. The selection of cribs was nearly overwhelming. We quickly passed the ornately painted models with scrollwork and wrought-iron accents, settling on a simple design made of beautiful, durable maple. It was huge in our bedroom — the only new piece of furniture we owned. That alone made it seem large. With Casey inside, it seemed to take up the entire apartment. Nearly five years worth of rocking it back and forth and the joints are still tight. The clear satin finish is unblemished after countless hours of leaning my face against the top rail. I should have known from the start — as soon as it became a fixture in our lives, as soon as it got familiar, the boys would chuck it over their shoulders and never look back. It can be a problem when you stop to consider the meaning of things: right now it's up, and there is a baby in the house. You can see it in the window from the road. You see it from a car through the old glass panes, glowing in the nightlight. A baby in this house. That's just not something I'm willing to give up yet. Not today.

I put the drill on a high shelf and head out in the truck with the boys — anything to keep from just standing in their room, mourning the past. For years now, I've driven by a hand-painted sign that points the way to what is described as a living historical farm. The day seems right for a visit. At the moment, I don't know just how right it is. The boys are working one of their lessons on me. Owen has laid the groundwork with the easy pass-off of his crib. Now it's Casey's turn to drive the point home.

"My, is it ever nice to see all of you," the old woman says. "So nice to get a visit. Especially from you young'uns." Casey and Owen glance at me. I nod. Yes, boys, she means you. It appears you're both young'uns in here. We're sitting on various stumps of wood with a small tour group in the middle of a turn-of-the-century Pennsylvania Standard: a large, overhanging barn built into the side of a hill. Admission tags hang from our shirt buttons. The old woman sits on a stump at the front of the group. She wears a long prairie dress and flat black leather shoes. Her head is covered with a billowy white bonnet. "Y'all can jes' call me 'Ma,'" she says. "What everyone calls me around here. You from the city?" Her neck juts forward and her eyes bug out as she looks to each of us. "Well, are ya?" she asks me. I don't know exactly what I'm supposed to say. A group of geese in the far corner unleash a deafening chorus of screeching. Owen flies into my lap. *"Oh, don't mind them,"* the woman shouts over the birds as they race around the group and into the barnyard. "Anyway, I was gonna say," she continues, "if y'all are from the city, I sure hope you brought along some tradin' goods. We're gettin' mighty low on tea and sugar around here, and Pa could sure use some new shoe leather afore the winter."

"Excuse me —" Casey says politely.

"Hold on, young'un," she says, her eyes wide and wild looking, a knobby index finger held in front of her looking very much as if it should have a poison apple dangling from it. Casey's mouth snaps shut. "Now, you listen to what I'm a gonna tell you — y'all listen. My granddaddy came to settle in these here hills *way* back. I was just a baby then but sometimes it's like it were yesterday. Hard times. Yes sir. That was before we had any of the modern conveniences we got today — the apple press, brick oven, butter churn — all the things that make gettin' by so easy now."

"Excuse me —" Casey says again.

The woman looks at him without missing a beat. "Young'un, do you know it used to take Pa six hours to make a hearth broom, but with the machine he got last year he can make over a dozen in one day? Sometimes I can't believe the changes." She slaps her leg and lets out a hoot. I understand what she's trying to do, but it's hard for me to play along — illusions don't come easy in a small town. I'm almost positive I saw old Ma cruising the bread machine aisle of the local Wal-Mart just last week.

"Excuse me," Casey tries again.

The woman stutters but continues her patter. Casey persists. She stops and turns to look at him with an eyebrow held high, "What's botherin' you, young'un?"

"Where do you have your computer at?" he asks. The group hushes. The word "computer" seems to echo from the old-growth ridge beams and purloin struts straight out to rattle the historically accurate cross-rail fencing along the perimeter of the farm. The woman shoots him a strained grin. I have a sudden urge to apologize.

"Young'un, I don't know what you're talkin' about," she says slowly. Casey's eyebrows go down.

"A *computer*," he says impatiently. "Where do you have your *computer*? You know."

"I *don't* know young'un," the woman says on the verge of a reprimand, the look in her eyes about as friendly as an underdone piece of chicken. "Whatever that thing is you're talkin' 'bout . . . we don't have 'em here." She gives me a glance and I know that one more modern reference out of Casey and she'll call the bouncer.

"Casey," I whisper in his ear. "The lady is pretending it's a long time ago. There weren't any computers back then."

"Why?" he whispers back.

"They weren't invented yet."

"What does 'invented' mean?"

"Tell you later."

We're subjected to a few more minutes of Ma's edgy nostalgia before being handed off to a more convincing "Pa," who, after a quick demonstration of mortise-and-tenon joinery and a dog-powered butter churn, brings us outside to a handsomely built smokehouse.

"This is where we preserve our meat," he announces plainly. Pa's beard is long and white, low on his cheeks and squared off on the bottom. His pants are held up with suspenders. He wears a crisp white shirt and a straw hat with a flat brim that looks handmade. "As far as I know, humans are the only creatures on earth that can tolerate the taste of smoke." He opens the door and a light blue cloud floats out. A split of apple wood sits on a small bed of coals. Pa takes a stick and pushes the ashes up around the log until it's almost covered. Plumes of sweet-smelling smoke rise to the ceiling, where all varieties of meat hang, wrapped with twine. He unhooks one half of a very large trout and brings it down for our approval. The smoke is working on it nicely. "I'd love to give each of you a taste," Pa says. "But it needs another three weeks before it's cured. Then it will be as good this December as the day in July when I pulled it from the stream."

"Excuse me," Casey says. "Can you make SpaghettiOs in this house?" Pa knows better than to feign eighteenth-century ignorance.

"SpaghettiOs might be difficult to do in here," he says with a sly smile as he hangs the trout back on the rail.

"Well, how about — can you make a pizza then?" Pa leans down into Casey's face.

"Tell you what, young man, do you like hot dogs?" Casey nods. "Hot dogs are good, right?"

"Sure."

"Well, we could make up a real fine hot dog in here," he says and then looks up to me with the same sly smile. "Only take about a month to do it."

We move on to the spinning and weaving rooms of an old

chinked log house. Casey takes in most of the demonstration before politely asking the weaver if her loom can make an alien suit. She makes the mistake of going into a big production about not knowing what an alien is. And she's about as stubborn as he is. I step in and change the subject before one of them resorts to blows.

In the candle-making shop, a young girl in bonnet and prairie dress begins her demonstration. "I'm so busy! We're running low on tallow candles — they take all day to make and burn up in twenty minutes! Oh, how I wish we had beeswax. The flame burns so much longer. The trader will come to visit soon and he may have some in his wagon. What kind of candles do you use in your bedrooms at night?" she asks buoyantly.

"Flashlight," Casey says flatly.

"Flashlight?" She lets out a long, artificial laugh. "Whatever could you mean, young'un?" she asks, assuming a sudden, alacritous hint of British accent.

"A flashlight."

"*Flashlight!* Is that how you say it? Is that how you say the word? My! I should very much like to see one some day. It sounds fancy — you must be from the city!" Casey looks up at me, bewildered.

In the parlor, he tries to talk the presenter into playing "Winnie-the-Pooh" on her pedal organ. She smiles and opts for a slow version of "Amazing Grace." All the verses. The boys are not impressed. This time, I apologize.

Standing in front of two massive Clydesdale horses, a thin woman in wire-rim glasses extolls their extraordinary strength and their ability to drag entire trees through the forest — *"Like a bulldozer!"* Owen cheers. But you get the picture.

A whole day of throwing stones into the eyes of history. I don't know where I got the idea that they could honor hand-made tester and trundle beds when they can't even muster the reverence to recognize the passing of their own crib. Casey and Owen do so naturally what is becoming increasingly difficult for me as I grow older. It's the blessed arrogance of their youth that enables them to always move forward. From a horse-drawn plow to their very own crib, the boys will never look back at the cost of looking ahead. Not even for a moment. Because the one thing about looking back is that you have to stand still to do it. Children don't stand still. And so it's life's perfect design that at thirty-five years old, I should get mixed up with these two and their healthy disrespect for antiquity — one that forces me at every turn to recognize the distinction between honoring the past and living in it.

As we leave the farm, walking through the charmed wooden gates and back to our truck, it strikes me that so much about the past is romanticized. It's the thing that makes every generation's older folks so certain their younger folks are going to the dogs. Even though I'd never say it out loud and hardly believe it in the first place, after the quiet day of apple butter, home-grown honey, and needlepoint, I can barely deny the chorus running through my head — *man, those were the days.* But it's far too easy to wax quixotic about the past while ignoring the disasters. A sign pointing the

way to the parking lot advertises an upcoming harvest festi-
val with "Tasty country foods! Folk entertainment! Quilt-
ing!" A truer depiction of the times would include a small
cabin next to the merry stone wall — reenactors sick in bed
with smallpox and rheumatic fever and a small cemetery for
children alongside the rustic springhouse.

Even the best of things during the best of times — if they
can't be brought to relevance in the present day, then they're
nothing more than relics. It's easy to see the grace of the
morning sun casting its long shadows across a small pasture,
but if that grace exists at all it can be found in every place. If
the wisdom of old exists at all, its truth applies to every age.
So many times when we hearken back to the virtues of the
past, we're only circling the wagons against modern-day
challenges that must be faced today. The common sense exchanged across a rustic stone fireplace, the peace that's found
in a horse-drawn carriage — those are easy. But they have
to survive the trip into the present. We have to be able to
take them home. Casey and Owen wouldn't miss any of it.
It's just that they know without ever being told that truth
and wisdom are limited only by our expectations of where
they reside, and that anything worth finding in the past can
be found, too, in today.

The crib is standing when Susan comes home from
work. She doesn't say a word about it that night as she tucks
Owen in, raising the rail and fluffing the coats piled high on
his landing pad. Several weeks later, it's gone. It seems right,
somehow, that if the father is the one to put it up, then it's

the mother who takes it down. I walk into the room and the Jenny Lind bed from the barn is standing in its place. Owen crawls into it that night as if it's been up for years. When I ask him if he likes it, his lip curls up — just the slightest bit proud.

Later on, before turning in, I stand in the doorway and watch him toss through the tangle of his blankets. The baby is suddenly gone. I never took my eyes from him — it happened while I was watching and I never saw it. He's stretched across the mattress, his body long, the days of curling into a fat little ball with his ankles to his chest abruptly behind him. No longer content with a foot in his mouth, no more pat-a-cake or this-little-piggy — when he rolls to the edge of the bed with the sunrise and puts his feet to the floor, he'll be strictly tic-tac-toe and stuck-in-the-mud. We didn't take a crib from a baby, we gave a bed to a boy. And it's all the example I need, to understand that honoring the things from the past that have brought us to where we are today is perfectly fine, as long as we acknowledge that those things alone could never keep us here.

The single bed, like his brother's now, says as much as anything else in the room — there are children in this house. That's something I'm willing to accept tonight. Not that it matters to him. I'm just trying to keep up. His next move will come as soon as I get comfortable, and I won't see it until it's already happened.

I'm fine with that. I have to be.

THE SOMERSAULT

The actual conversation is quite logical, the arguments reasoned and specific. The tone is congenial, inquisitive — not at all revealing of the sheer zaniness of what we're actually talking about. It's Casey who started it all, though Owen's quick contributions help move the whole thing along quite nicely. He bears some of the responsibility.

The topic is speed. The question is, which is faster, rain, bullets, or turkeys. Within the walls of a child's mind, the answer is not so certain. A bullet — very fast, the first logical choice, is open to debate. Rain, Casey points out, falling from a very high cloud and pushed along by a tornado, would move extremely fast. Owen is the romantic, the independent. He casts his vote for the turkey.

"Faster than a bullet?" I ask him. He nods — your average turkey on your average day: faster than a bullet. Casey asks what I think. I tell him I guess a bullet is faster than rain or turkeys.

"What about a tiny bullet?" Owen asks.

"Yeah — a really tiny bullet," Casey says. "Is rain faster than a very, very tiny bullet?" I tell him I'm pretty sure any bullet would be faster than a raindrop.

"What about a turkey?" Owen shoots.

"Turkey too."

"What about a really big turkey?" he shoots again. "A really, really fast — *really* big turkey?"

"Yeah," Casey says. "What about a really big turkey that's very, *very* fast."

"Bullet's faster," I say.

"A supersmall bullet," Casey tries.

"Faster."

Owen lights up. *"What about a red turkey?"* he says.

"Faster."

The line of inquiry goes along much farther than anyone would ever believe. Only after we've nailed down every hypothetical loose end do I realize how effortlessly they've waltzed me down the rabbit hole. The boys have brought us back and through the looking glass so many times now, I've lost track of which side we're on. It's why I can carry on a serious conversation with Casey while he's balancing an orange on his head, why Owen curling up and falling asleep on a small end table is perfectly fine with me. You come to our house and you'd like to put a foot in the toilet? I have no problem with that. You'd suddenly like to know how many buttons fit in your nose? I understand. I am not the least bit fazed. Go right ahead. Give me the final count — I'll post the tally on the fridge next to the painting of a dinosaur lounge act in outer space. I'll read it out loud over a pickle-and Ice Pop dinner in my best Elmer Fudd voice to Susan and the boys in pajamas and cowboy hats. We'll have a laugh and pour a milkshake into the stereo for you.

I surrendered a long time ago.

The coherence gluing one minute to the next has dissolved. Place settings and table arrangements are absent — even the idea of them, even the hope of them. Detailed, synchronous adult conversations exist only in memory. But when I miss these things most, I try to remember that they will all return one day, and the children who've tipped them over will be gone forever. It works for me most of the time, but some days I'd really just like to have a dinner where I didn't have to jump up to help someone use the toilet.

After buttoning down the corners of the bullet-rain-turkey question, the boys exchange a nod as if some small piece of the world has been clarified. They run off down the lawn. I retreat to a pile of oak logs that need splitting, pounding through the big red monsters, holding every fourth or fifth split to my nose. Better than apple pie and better than bacon. If there's a smell in Heaven, it has to be the smell of red oak. Halfway through the pile, Casey comes running up the hill with a sudden announcement.

"I can do a somersault now," he says, the words leaping from his mouth, his eyes shooting upward in their sockets, too eager for my approval to receive it head-on.

"You can?" I ask. He nods quickly, still unable to look at my face. His shoulders are high with the pride of even being able to say he's completed this milestone.

"I just did it — just now," he says, a little out of breath because he knows what he's actually saying is that he just became a full-fledged kid. In the blink of an eye. There would be no arguing it now; a somersault proves it.

"With Owen?"

"By myself."

"By yourself."

"I was on the lawn and I did it," he says and nods his head silently before finally glancing at my face.

"Wow," I say, one word like a match that lights the candles behind his eyes. He shoots them to the sky, still unable to gaze directly at my approval.

"Want to see it?" he asks as the brightness fills his face. In an instant I can see the lengths he would travel for my approval — the mountains he would climb so that I might say, "Wow" or "Good job," and mean it. The words mean so much more than they actually should, but there is no escaping this pedestal he's put me on. He did a somersault by himself but has to do it for me to make it real. It's an aspect of parenting I hadn't considered when Susan and I were deciding to have children. We knew about the sleepless nights and the diapers — people had told us about colic and all the rest, but the one thing they all forgot to mention was that the biggest thing that comes with a newborn, along with the lower-back pain and friendly glances of total strangers, is power. Overwhelming and absolute power. Even if you never see it coming. Even if it's the last thing you're worthy to hold.

"Do you want to see one, Dad?" Casey asks again. "Want to see me do a somersault?" He looks at me as though I could shower him with the world.

"Yeah, I do, Casey," I say. The candles flash brilliantly behind his eyes. A part of me wants to swallow his adoration
whole, but another side wants to tell him to get a grip on himself — it's just me here —*just your father, you know? I'm not
half the man you think I am. Please take some of this back because I don't actually deserve it. I should tell you so that you
won't find out one day and be disappointed — I should tell you
right up front, Casey — I'm just a guy. I'm doing my best, but
that's all I'm doing. Sometimes it's enough. Many times it isn't.*

It wouldn't change a thing if I actually said it. Even on the
days when I have nothing, even when I'm flat on my back,
he finds a way to look up to me. He tugs my arm. Tells me
to c'mon. I lay the maul on its side against the pile of logs
and we walk down the hill toward a soft spot in the grass.
Owen rides my shoulders. He picks wood chips from my
hair and runs his palms over the stubble of my cheeks. I remember doing the same with my father when he was so much
more than just a guy — when the feel of his rough beard
was like that of a huge, hairy god and, riding on his shoulders, I could bury my face into his scalp or reach up to run
my fingers through the stars. Casey's shoulders are high
with the pride of what he's about to show me. As we walk, I
feel a slow expansion into the image they hold of me — an
image that carries with it the expectation of delivery. The
boys have left me no choice. For an instant, I am every bit
the hero they believe me to be. If Casey needs my witness to
make a somersault real, then I can do that. If Owen thinks a
shoulder ride and two-day beard are just this side of heaven,
then today it's true. For this brief moment, I hold the power
on the floodgates of the world — with a touch, I'm able to

send it showering down around them. All they have to do is ask. All they have to do is believe that I can.

In a previous life as an emergency-shift social worker in a large Manhattan hospital, I worked during the night and on weekends, when the regular staff was off. My job was to resolve all nonmedical problems, most having to do with discharge planning that involved girls in their late teens and early twenties who'd just given birth to their third or fourth child from a third or fourth father. It was usually a nurse who called me to the floor so that I might have a conversation with the young mother about her preparations for the newborn and then, also, try to broach the subject of the wonders of the modern world and this thing we all call birth control. Most of the girls I talked with swore up and down to me that the baby in their arms was their last, that things would be different the next time, for some reason. And I'd see them again, ten or twelve months later — another baby at their breast, another promise on their lips.

Some of the girls, who were more honest with me and with themselves, would just look out the window when I asked if the baby lying across their arms was the last. They knew that it should be — knew that it could be — but also knew that no matter what they said to me or what I said to them, there was something bigger than the two of us at play here, something with the momentum of the earth's rotation that would roll them back into the maternity floor like the change of seasons. I was familiar with much of what the professional journals had to say about the problem of young, single mothers of numerous children — explanations that usually boiled down to some variation of the girl's desperate search for "unconditional love" from a man and then, when that failed, his child. But whenever I left these girls, that explanation never seemed to entirely cover it. There was something else going on here, something more than the desire to feel needed by a child or loved for an instant by a man who never spends the night.

There was a girl with a look in her eyes, one Saturday afternoon, that said it all. I had gone through my usual routine, clipboard in one hand, hospital chart in the other, different-colored pen behind each ear, clinic IDs around my neck, beeper buzzing madly at my hip, a nice watch, crisp shirt and jacket and shoes and twill pants with cuffs of the proper width — all the pieces of a person accustomed to some measure of power. You know the type — thirty years old and the world by the tail and fresh off a flashy morning conversation with friends who use words like *moxie* and *doppelgänger* to describe everyday events. I had rolled in with all the arrogant presumption of someone who has it made and begun a line of questioning that probably sounded more like an interrogation — the essence of which amounted to something like, *Why on earth do you keep having babies with no possible way of supporting them?* And the girl sized me up and turned slowly to the window, the look in her eyes saying, *How you gonna understand the answer, Mister, when you don't even understand the question? How you gonna ask me that, when you're never gonna understand what it's like to have nothing — what it's like when having nothing is all anyone in your family going all the way back has ever known — what it's like to know there's no hope of escaping it? You wanna try and understand what that's like? Because then you gotta imagine what happens when having nothing makes the shift into* being *nothing. And when being nothing makes the shift into being invisible. You think you can understand what it's like to disappear? Have you ever looked into the mirror and found there wasn't anything there?*

No, I didn't think so.

So many times, it seems the divide across the nation is nothing more than the people with everything wondering why on earth the people with nothing do the things they do. Only this afternoon as the boys gaze up at me from the grass, do I begin to understand the real question — not *How could you keep having babies?* but *When the rest of the world no longer believes in you, how could you possibly stop?* Children will find your brilliance. Where there is none — they will create it. How could anyone possibly resist that?

As I look at Casey and Owen, their eyes shower me with adornments. I am Hercules — descendent of Zeus — conqueror of the twelve labors. I am Superman. I am actually made of steel. I am the almighty protector — no harm can come to those who are with me. I am the strongest, fastest, most intrepid warrior on the planet. I know everything. I see everything. All that I say is true. I heal cuts and bruises. I fix any toy. I make the best jelly sandwiches. Only when I turn away from them do I become just a guy — so familiar with my own failings and weaknesses that I can barely see beyond them. I turn back and I'm suddenly the arbiter of all things, the godlike filter through which everything passes.

I could never be as good as they believe me to be. But it's their belief that makes me want to try. There are moments when I get close to it — brief periods when I'm every bit of what they have made me out to be. I'm a better person at these moments than I've ever been at any other time in my life. Because of them. Because they have made me so.

The simple lesson is one they have demonstrated every second of every day from the first moment they were born. For all the times that I've begged and cajoled the important people in my life to step up to the plate when I needed them most, I wish I had known what Casey and Owen have known from the very start: *if you need someone to be brilliant, believe first that they are.* I would have never thought it was that simple had it not worked so well on me. It's something I want to remember, so when the boys are grown and reconciled to the fact that I'm no Hercules, I can still reach down and pull things out that are so divine they have no business coming out of this flawed, mortal soul. If I forget everything else, I will always remember this: when I need to find that spark of brilliance in myself, the first thing I will do is find the person who already sees it there.

Casey asks Owen and me if we're ready. His face is serious. The first somersault is a sober, concentrated affair. A moment you can't step back from. I tell him we're ready. He takes a quick breath and sends his legs arcing through the air. The top of his head twists into the grass. His neck bends under the strain of his upturned body. He rolls to his shoulder, does a half twist, and flattens onto the ground. That wasn't it. He tells us to just-wait-just-wait-just-wait as he crouches his body and lowers his head to the grass. He kicks his legs skyward. They freeze at the apex, list right, flutter, and fall back to the ground. That wasn't it either — just-wait-just-wait. He shoots them again. And then again. Forget the fact that a spinning, spread-eagle handstand is infinitely more impressive than a simple somersault — just-wait-just-wait, he says, that wasn't it. He shoots his legs back and up one more time, a little harder now. They pinwheel like a mad break-dancer's, pulling him spectacularly sideways — his torso spiraling left and then compensating right — feet pedaling against the clouds, palms pushing back the ground, elbows wobbling, neck teetering, until the whole works lurch blindly forward and over to a hard-fought completion. Owen and I cheer.

"Did I do it?" Casey asks, his eyes wide and bewildered.

"You did it!" I yell.

"You saw me do it?"

"I did, Casey! I saw you do it!" Only then does the satisfaction rush to his face.

"I can do a somersault?"

"You can. You can do a somersault, Casey."

"You saw me do it."

"I saw you do it."

Owen gives one a try but can't get it done. A couple of fancy-looking rolls but no somersault, thank heaven — not the hard-jaw, slap-shot kid just yet, he's still the tumbling, bumbling child. I don't think I could take another first-time somersault in one day. After several more tries, he gives up and lies still on his back under the trees. I walk over and sit in the grass next to him. We watch his brother, like an un-coordinated modern dancer, slowly somersault over to join us. Then I tuck the two of them into my chest and roll us down the hill. Their hoots and squeals of laughter are as if I'm showering them with the world. They tell me to do it again, they say they want more. Every child asks for the world, every parent can give it to them. It's just that the world they ask for has nothing to do with anything that can be bought — nothing to do with anything outside of your own four walls. Casey and Owen's faces blur as they tumble around me. I am their world. I'm shining in their eyes and raining down around them like thunder. I'm laid at their feet — the ground all around them — the sky and the moon and the stars, and I can give it all. I can give them their fa-ther. Susan can give them their mother. We can give them the world.

The three of us, dizzy and out of breath, come to a stop under two large maples at the bottom of the hill. The only sound is breathing as we look up through the canopy of leaves. Casey nestles his head on my shoulder. Owen crawls up to rest his cheek against my chest. Only a memory could be as sweet. A light breeze swings the branches through the sky, and I wonder, *would the trees, if they could, think every cloud a hero? Would they call every drop of rain brilliance? Every ray of light a savior? Would the rain and the sun be those things without the trees to make them so?*

But there's no time for an answer.

"Daddy?" Casey suddenly asks, "what if the turkey was in a racer car? Then would it be the fastest?"

"A *red* turkey," Owen fires, and we're back down the

rabbit hole to shuffle the pieces of the bullet-rain-turkey question, the boys rearranging the parts until the bullet finally loses the race — the rain is in a hurricane, the bullet *underwater,* and the *red* turkey in a race car. They ask me to sign off on it, and when I do, it becomes law.

THE TROUT

The guy at the bait shop thinks I've got a secret. I do, but it's not the one he's thinking. I've been coming in for minnows for the last two weeks. Really big minnows. Borderline pan fish.

"You got any that are bigger than these?" I ask. His net in the tank, he looks at me as if I asked for a tarpon.

"Bigger?"

"Right, bigger."

"Where in the hell are you fishin' at, guy?" I laugh and nod, for some reason. The man just stares. He wants an answer.

"Oh, just around," I say. "You know. Here and there."

"And you want something bigger than these right here?"

"Right."

"Guy — nobody is pullin' minnows like these yet. It's too early. Where in the hell are you — wait a minute." He pulls the net out of the tank, holding it in front of his face. A four-inch shiner flexes in the webbing. "You want bigger than this one right here?"

"Right," I say. "If you've got any."

"Well, I sure wish I knew where in the hell you were fishin' at —"

"I think there are bigger ones at the bottom of this tank over here," I say, and can't help noticing a few of the regulars casually eyeing me. One of them looks out the window to see what I'm driving.

"You were in three days ago, weren't you?" the owner asks, stepping around the boys and up to the tank.

"Yeah. Was it just three days ago?"

"Yeah, it was three days ago. I remember thinking, cripes — wonder where in the hell that guy's fishin' at."

"Yeah."

"You know?"

"Sure."

"Shit, guy — where in the hell are you using this kind of bait around here?"

I'd tell him, only I think it might be illegal. And I'd hate to disappoint him. It's sure to be a topic of discussion at the local bar; they'll all have more fun with it if they don't know the truth.

I pay the man — three dollars for two bags of fish. I strap the boys in their seats and put a bag in each of their laps. By the time we get home, they're still staring at them. Owen says his bag tickles. We take them up the hill and dump them into a large, shallow pail. The boys pull up their sleeves and roll their arms through them. When they tire of that, we take the pail over to a deep spot in the stream and tip them in. Wire netting downstream from the pool keeps them from floating away. They school into the face of the current as soon as they hit the water. The boys sit on the bank and throw sinking pellets just ahead of them, thrilling when they dart forward to snap them up. In a moment, they have turned from bait fish into pets.

Or so it seems.

We walk up to the small pool several days later to find half of our little pets replaced by a fat brown snake as close to smiling as I've ever seen one. The following day there are two snakes, both smiling. The fish are gone. Calling them pets doesn't take the bait out of the bait fish. Casey suggests another round. Owen agrees, and so we head out for more — a different shop this time, before the people at the old one begin to suspect I'm using them in sandwiches.

We get two more bags from the sporting goods shop in town with a lot fewer questions, take them home, and tip them in. Casey and Owen push sticks slowly through the school, with only an occasional pleading on my part that they do so nicely. And then they settle on their stomachs to simply watch. There is a lot on display in a three-dollar bag of minnows, a lot to learn about — fear, perseverance, flight, pursuit, daring, nuance — it's all there once you pour the bag into a small, deep pool and take the time to find it. But then there has to be more — always more when there are children with you — always — what's next and let's go and c'mon and do it.

"You haven't taken your boys fishing yet?" a friend of mine asks one day. We're on the topic of my disappearing bait fish, and he tells me as surely as the boys have that I have to take the exercise further. His own son can barely hold his head up and has been fishing almost as much as he's been breastfed. "The streams in your area are packed with trout," he says. He's incredulous. He threatens to call the authorities so that the boys are taken from me and given to a man who would hand them a pole. It's the time-honored father-and-child activity, he says, the thing that links all ages of man to one another. Women have childbirth, men have fishing. Unequal as they may be, the two are the same for all people for all time — two activities that will never change. All right, all right, I tell him. "Anyway," he says, "they'll just love it. You'll love it too. You just take them fishing. You don't ask why. That's the best way."

He may be right about the universal sanctity of the father-and-child fishing trip. One of my earliest memories of my dad is of the two of us in a boat on a cold Minnesota morning. But who doesn't have at least a few fishing stories that would hold the attention of any given gathering around the campfire? The only problem with my stories is that in most of them, no fish are caught. I don't know what we were fishing for but remember ripping my hook through the mouths of at least a half-dozen fish. *A little softer,* Dad told me. But the next nibble and twitch in the pole triggered my young arms like the spring in a mouse trap. Another bite and a smack of the reel against my forehead, then one more time — a fish with an extraordinarily strong mouth that I jerked overhead and then back again before Dad put a stop to it, lunging forward and wrapping me with his arms like you would a crazed gunman or suicide jumper.

We didn't have any fish by the end of the morning, so Dad stopped at a lakefront shop and picked out a couple of foot-long beauties to take home for the frying pan. He sat them in my lap for the drive home. I looked at their eyes through the plastic wrapping, then put my finger in the mouth of one for some reason — an invitation for the fish to exact the smallest revenge through the plastic, and it did. I was bitten.

At ten years old, I taught my youngest sister everything I knew about fishing, and it nearly killed her. We walked back to the river behind our house, where she caught about seven small, wholly inedible fish with crooked spines and spots on their fins. I made her string them through the gills with a sprig of willow and take them back to the house, where she gutted each one in the sink before turning a sudden shade of yellow and heading for the bathroom. She became a vegetarian shortly after the experience and remains so to this day — a condition I have to take credit for along with Colonel Sanders and the limp vein that snapped back from a chicken leg as she bit into it.

"The trout by you have no idea what a fly is," my friend tells me. "Don't bother getting mixed up in all the hype about nymphs and gnats and woollies. Most of your trout are hatchery — they see a Cahill or Blue Dun on the water and couldn't care less about it. Throw something that looks like a food pellet or a piece of corn and they go crazy." He does most of his fishing in northern California, and I feel a sudden patriotism about the Pennsylvania trout — hatchery or not. I want to defend their standing in the trout continuum but have nothing in the way of experience to back my conviction. Pennsylvania trout grab ass and swill bad gin for all I know.

"And don't bother getting all the *stuff*," he tells me. What stuff? I ask him. "The *stuff* — all the stuff. The world of trout fishing is very laden with stuff. I see guys up here in their six-mil neoprene waders, everything under the sun dangling from their hat and vest — they bounce into the stream like golden retrievers and the fish scatter. They don't care, these guys — they're not there for fish, it's just a gear-fest for them. They just wanna use their stuff. They got the forty-four million modulus graphite, fast taper rod with the one-way, clutch-bearing, Teflon-impregnated cork-disk drag reel — costs as much as their SUV for chrissake — loaded up with synthetic-coated, laser-jet-painted copolymer multi-strand hot-wax line, and who cares if there's a fish at the end of it — you know? It's a sickness. Don't let anyone tell you you need all the stuff. Just go fishing. Don't get the fluorocarbon tippet threader. Don't get the breast-pocket barometer."

He knows what he's talking about. His garage-sale pole, "the feather that would haul a monster," he says — has done him years of good service. Any good friend knows your weakness, and most of mine know that I have a tendency to be seduced by stuff. Even as he's casting the gear guys as victims and suckers, I'm thinking, *breast-pocket barometer? Hey — I could use one of those.*

"What you do —" my friend says in a low voice. "Find

out about a good stream. That's the main thing. Ask around. You find out where they're running. Then take the boys and any old pole and head out — real early if you can, but don't worry if it's later. Okay. Stop about twenty feet from the stream and get right on the ground. Tell the guys to be quiet. Tell them to whisper. Then you take a piece of Wonder bread out of your pocket — that's right: Wonder bread. I don't care what anyone says — you take off the crust, rip it into quarters, roll a piece into a ball, and put it on your hook. Wonder bread *will* catch fish. Now listen; you have to crawl up to the stream. Get everyone right down on their bellies with their heads low. Creep right up on it — nice and easy, then roll to your side and toss the bread ball over your head like a grenade into the water. Man, that's the way you do it. If there's a trout in there, he'll hit it."

My friend, sinewy and windblown in dungarees and a faded plaid shirt, is the ultimate man of the forest streams — as wild and beautiful as the trout he's after. I don't doubt that he could bring me to tears with a demonstration of his unique brand of fishing, but for me to take it on would be like the plus-size girl who buys a miniskirt because it looks good on the ninety-pound model. And I know who I am — more pocket barometer than pocket of Wonder bread. I'd be willing to give it a try if I were certain that no one would catch me doing it. But then with children, you always run the risk that something you do could get locked into their permanent memory and come back to haunt you later on. I'm not so sure I want to take the chance that twenty years from now, Casey and Owen would remember lying on their backs, throwing bread balls into a stream and then decide to ask with an adult's scrutiny, just exactly what I was thinking — *So Dad, we were talking with some friends and they said their fathers used to take them fishing in* boats. *They used* worms *for bait. Anyway . . . you wanna tell us what was up with the GI crawl and the Wonder bread?*

I'm not going to crawl on hands and knees around any stream beds, but I'm in agreement that the good father does more than throw a bucket of bait into the water and call it a day of fishing. Luckily, our neighbors down the road have generously offered the services of their fully stocked trout pond, where on a bad day when the fish are not biting, every tenth cast gets a hit. I turn to Casey and Owen one afternoon with the shadows getting long and nothing planned for supper. "You two want to go fishing?" I ask.

"Sure," Casey says plainly.

"Owen?" He stands up from the sandbox, nodding.

"Sure," he says, and we're off, headfirst into the long tradition of life's richest treasures springing out of a day of fishing. Most everyone who has ever tried it, from the dabbler to the lifer, is compelled at some point to draw a conclusion or two about their existence and the way it all goes. I think it could be inevitable that the longer you live, the greater the probability that you'll see something in a day of fishing that will bring you to your knees. I load the boys into the truck and the pole into the back next to a white enameled pail for holding our catch. I light the coals on the grill in an act of blind optimism, and as we head out, it all feels so right that I can't imagine why I haven't done it sooner.

"All right boys," I say, opening the tackle box. "Choose

your poison." The three of us are on our knees along a grassy bank. The sun is low at our backs, casting its ocherous warmth against the facing hills. "Owen, you're first. What would you like to use?" His eyes pore carefully over the selection. I lift the tray to reveal a second tier of tackle — most of it bright and shining, woefully underused. As Owen considers the choices, I'm suddenly struck by the similarities of a tackle box and a jewelry box — both of them the same size, with sectioned-off compartments, both filled with lures, colorful and sparkling — the tackle with hooks, the jewelry without — although just as easy to get snagged on should you get mixed in one dangling from a vanilla-scented earlobe. It seems right that boxes holding earrings and earwigs should be so similar.

"Pick one, Owen," I say.

"Umm . . ."

"Which one will catch a big ol' fish?"

"This one!" he chimes, holding up a bobber.

"Oh — not a bobber, Owen."

"Why not a bobber?"

"Because you can't catch a fish with a bobber."

"But I *want* the bobber," he whines.

"Pick another one, Owen." His face and shoulders fall dramatically. "Look at this," I say. "Look — there's no hook on a bobber, see? Choose something with a hook on it so we can catch a fish."

"But Daddy — *I really want to use this bobber.*"

"Owen."

"*Right now* — I really want to use it."

"Owen —"

"I *do*."

"Okay, take the bobber — here. You can play with it. Casey's turn!"

"*Daddy* —" Owen cries. "*I want the bobber on that fishing pole — right now —*"

"Owen, which lure do you think Casey is gonna choose?" Owen throws his bobber to the ground, collapsing in despair. Casey scans both tiers of the tackle box and then cuts his eyes briefly at mine. He chooses a bobber.

I try the whole thing again. I tell them we're fishing. I tell them you try to catch fish when you go fishing. I tell them fish are not attracted to bobbers. But it's no use. Given a choice of any kind, children will always select the thing that is most like a ball or piece of candy. In a tackle box, lying amidst chub grubs and scum frog poppers, the candy-apple-red-and-peppermint-white bobber is really the only choice.

As I tie the bobber to the end of the line along with a few sinkers so I'm able to cast it out, I look over my tackle box at some of the more elaborate lures that have never fulfilled the promise of their flash. And for all the times I threw them without a strike, I might as well have been throwing a bobber. I'm pretty convinced your average decent, hardworking fish finds several of my lures repulsive, frightening even. I keep them all the same — throwing them out when all other reasonable measures have failed, on the chance that a twenty-pounder lurks on the bottom with a taste that leans toward the kinky. *The gentlefish would care for a bug-eyed extraterrestrial go-go dancer in Day-Glo pink, perhaps?* I wouldn't be at all surprised if there was a ridiculous-looking lure in every tackle box — one that has never attracted a fish but will never be thrown away. The lure with propellers. The singing lure. The scented lure. The strobe-light lure. Lures that look like psychedelic mobiles — like boomerangs and hairy vegetables and gelatinous, fluorescent-green shop tools. I might as well snip the hooks off some of mine for all the interest they've inspired. But I throw them — my own version of casting a bobber. Sometimes you just want to see something go through the water. Sometimes you just want to use your stuff.

I cast.

The bobber flies high and long, landing in the middle of the pond and floating on the surface. The boys think it's beautiful. I hand Casey the rod and show him how to bring it back. His eyes get thin with concentration as he reels it in. The bobber ducks just below the surface, its crisp black wake like an arrow pointing in our direction as it returns. I cast again. The sinkers rotate around the bobber like electrons as the whole mess soars through the air and hits the water with a splash. Owen brings it back this time, very slowly, his left fist pumping awkwardly around the reel. The smile never leaves his face. "Farther," Casey pleads, and so I haul off and throw the bobber as hard as I can. It shoots through the sky like a bottle rocket. The boys let out a breath. They clap when it lands. They comment to each other about how far it went. "Is the bobber working?" Casey asks as he pulls it in. "It's working," I tell him. "Better than I've ever seen one work." He reels in a few more. Owen does too. No fish, but a fine evening of casting.

With light bleeding out of the sky, I ask the boys if it's my turn to choose a lure. They concede. There is so little time left, I look over the selection and decide to use a sure thing — the Armani of fishing lures — uncomplicated, refined, deadly. I choose a Phoebe. A simple curve of stamped brass with a treble hook at the tail; the humble Phoebe rarely fails to deliver. It's the cheese pizza of the fish world because just about every species will give it a bite. Rapalas are good — especially the small Fat Rap, but if I had to use a single lure for the rest of my life, I'd choose a Phoebe.

I cast — a quick side-arm flip of the pole that sends the lure on a short horizontal trip over the water before it slips under the dark surface with a soft sounding "gulp." I let it sink and then reel quickly, smoothly. It ripples on the surface as it nears the bank and then jingles up to the tip of the pole. The boys are not impressed. I cast again. The Phoebe skips lightly and slips under. I reel. In a moment, there is a silent, vigorous pull. "Here you go, Casey," I say, quickly handing him the pole. "Reel it in." His eyes startle and then light with determination as he realizes there's a fish on. He spins the reel furiously. The line pulls to the left and then arcs slowly to the right. The trout leaps into the air, its belly flashing the last traces of orange sunlight. A very nice fish. A perfect first fish. Nothing delivers in a pinch like a Phoebe.

Casey backs up as he reels until the fish is with us on the grass. I remove the hook and hold it up to the boys, who touch it with index fingers. I bring it over to the pail and drop it in. Casey and Owen crouch on either side to watch it flip through the water. I hook another and offer the pole to Owen but he prefers to watch. Then there are two fish in the pail. I catch one more for three in the pail and then bring them to the edge of the water to dress them out. Casey's trout is the largest. I clean it first. The boys watch quietly as I lay the brightly colored organs out for their inspection. They ask me to identify the pieces and I do the best I can. "Daddy, look —" Owen says suddenly, pointing to the middle of the pile. With the tip of my knife, I push back the other organs to reveal a beating heart. "It's *moving*," Casey says. The fish is in the pail but the heart is beating rhythmically in the grass. "Can we *look* at it?" Owen says. I cut it loose from the other organs and place it between them — a small, squeezing eraser head with a thin fatty crown. They are quickly lost in its spell.

By the time I've finished with the other two fish, Owen is off chasing a cat along the edge of a field. Casey hasn't moved. He's still watching. I go to the bank and dip my knife into the water to rinse it off. I dry the blade with the bottom of my shirt, fold it, and push it into my back pocket. Then I walk over to Casey, who is standing now, gazing into his hand. The small heart lies in his outstretched palm, squeezing slowly. Casey's face is somber, deeply serious. Then I feel the same seriousness in my face, and we're both swimming in the cool air of this oddly spiritual moment. I want to know what he's thinking — what his inner voice is telling him, but then I'm suddenly overtaken by the sight of this heart in his hand and its stunning portrayal of the relationship between the two of us. I'm suddenly overcome by my own inner voice —

It might as well be mine, Casey — that heart in your hand. Still beating, still alive, but no longer with me. No longer in my control. You took it when I wasn't watching, and I will never have it back. It will always belong to me, but it will always be with you. You will hold it when I'm joyful, you will hold it in my sorrow, you will hold it when I'm cruel to you, when I laugh with you, when I question you. Even when I don't understand you, you will still be holding my heart. It will be with you when I hold you up and when I let you down. And you will know me far better than I could ever know you, because you are holding and I am only being held.

Today, you hold it like a child, right up front. You hold it high for everyone to see. A stranger can glance at you and know that you are holding my heart. But you will have it even when you've put it behind you, when you grow older, and it's no longer the first thing you show to the world. You will have it even when it's hidden from everyone. Even when it's hidden from you. Even when it's hidden from me.

Then one day when you leave, you will take it with you. It will still belong to me. I will wait for its return because I will always need it. But I'll not see it again — not like this, not like today. And I'll feel the ache of every moment that it's gone. Some days the ache will bruise me and some days it will almost kill me, but it will never make me sorry, because I'll always know that it's the price I've paid to be held by you. It's the price I've paid for this blessed ride in the palm of your hand.

He looks up at me through his bangs. "I'm going to keep it," he says softly.

"I know, Case," I say. "I know you are."

He closes his hand around the heart and walks away from me, down to the water's edge. I load the pole, the tackle box, and the pail of fish into the truck. Then I sit on the tailgate and look out. Along the edge of a field, Owen is chasing the cat with a stick. Casey is sitting on the pond's bank, staring into the palm of his hand. The sun has ducked under the horizon — gone except for the few high clouds that are still bleeding red.

———

I'm the last one to sleep in this house.

On any given night, I can be found passing through the darkened, half-lit rooms — a witness to the unique peace of a home's secret life; rays of light from the moon or lamppost or a passing vehicle piercing through the windows at odd angles like a magician's swords through a Houdini box. The nightlight, invisible during the day, suddenly the focus of the room. The sound of the dog sleeping, the hum of the refrigerator, the scrape of branches — walls and surfaces and objects of a place so familiar, suddenly taking on new meaning. The path I take usually ends, as it has tonight, in Casey and Owen's bedroom, my last stop of the night to check on them. Check on what, I can't say exactly. It's usually no more than an adjustment of a sheet or blanket that's needed. I push an arm back where it belongs or a neck straight, maybe take the half-eaten cracker out of a half-open hand and put it on the dresser, but it always feels so much more important than that.

There is a chair in the corner of the room that faces their beds, the kind of chair and position in the room that makes you feel you should say something important when you sit in it. It has the slightest feel of a soapbox. I can only imagine the judgments I'll pronounce from this spot one day —

Casey and Owen seated at the end of their beds, listening intently, or only pretending to. Actually, this is the same chair Susan used to nurse the two of them, and as I sit here thinking about that, I can only hope that I will give them something as nourishing from this same spot one day.

They're breathing heavily now, the hall light streaming softly across their full bellies. They loved the trout. Susan loved hers too. The coals were almost out by the time we got home — perfect for the delicate meat of this delicate fish. Susan filled the body cavities with onions and butter, wrapped them in foil and nestled them into the embers. When they were cooked, we lifted the bones out and the boys ate them with a spoon. I loved my trout too, but for a different reason. I loved mine because Casey had held its heart and, in doing so, shed light into the essence of what it is to love him — what it is to love at all.

Before having children, I felt a certain invulnerability, a kind of deep, spiritual impenetrability that I had always considered a strength. Nothing could get to me. Nothing could slow me down. I had worked hard to achieve a level of inner stability that was reliable. It was safe. It's the way I wanted it. I felt the slow erosion of that safety when Susan became pregnant with Casey, an erosion that increased in perfect sync with the size of her belly. I didn't understand what it was at the time, I could only feel the change. Now I know that the feeling was that of my heart being taken away from me, eased from my grasp to be held by hands so much warmer but so much less secure than my own.

I had always believed that it was possible to retain the smallest piece of control when you fell in love — that you could do it without making the terrifying leap of actually handing over everything. But Casey and Owen have shown me it's futile to try and have it any other way. Love and terror ship in the same package. The two are inseparable. If it doesn't feel like something deep inside could crack at any minute, it's not love. So there are no such things as strong lovers — the truest lovers are walking day in and day out with a hole in their chests, scared as hell most of the time. I used to think of that kind of vulnerability as a weakness, but the boys have taught me that it's my strength — not something to be hidden, but something to be embraced — something to be held up high for all to see as the only proof and true measure of how hard I'm playing the game, of how much and how deeply I have loved.

The chair creaks as I get up to leave. Casey stirs and then begins a jumbled mash of small sentences. I walk over and cup my hand to the side of his face until he eases back into sleep. Owen rustles the blankets. His head is pushed sideways against the guardrail of his bed. I pull his thighs like the end of a sheet, to straighten him out. I string his favorite blanket through his half-open hand. Then I do something I've never done before. I lower my ear to his tiny chest and allow the sound of his heartbeat to fill my head. With my eyes closed, I listen to the beating rhythm mesh into the sound of my own breathing — the mechanics clicking between us like clockwork. His heart beats four times as I inhale and then six as I let it out. Four beats breathing in. Six beats breathing out. My head lightly rides the rise and fall of his chest. I want this to last forever. Four in. Six out. Four in. Six out. *Where are you off to, young man?* Four going into me. Six going out of me. *Why are you leaving?* Four steps closer. Six steps farther. *Where will I ever find you like this again? When will I ever know you this true?*

I lift my head and the beat stays with me. I walk out the door and it's still going strong. I hear it in the bed. I hear it in tomorrow.

And never be sorry for the price I've paid.

To hear it when he's gone.

THE WEED

Light a candle in the rain
Sing a sad song in the dark
Throw a flower in the river
In memory of my heart
— Julie and Buddy Miller

Somewhere along the middle of May, Susan pointed out one morning over coffee that we were already past the time when responsible parents of children Casey's age have applied, been registered, and had their child accepted into a school for the coming fall. The realization hit me as if she'd poured her coffee over my head. She was right. We were late. It had been a form of denial — enjoying a slow and sleepy spring without so much of a passing thought about preparations for the approaching fall.

"What were we thinking?" I asked.

"I know," she said.

"So what do we do, then?"

"Well, we have to get him in somewhere."

"Right, obviously," I said, getting short with her for no other reason than the onset of panic. She returned with a little of her own. We spun our wheels a few times before putting down our coffees and picking up the phone book.

There was the public school nearby, which was the obvious choice. Susan had visited when we were deciding whether or not to settle in the area. She had gone into the classrooms and looked through the textbooks to see whether or not the district had emerged from the dark ages of educational practice. It had, she decreed. But this was years ago, when the idea of depositing Casey into the jaws of the system was only theoretical.

I called the school. Yes, we were late, a woman told me. No, it wasn't exactly okay. Yes, they'd squeeze us into the final admissions group with the other parents who thought about their child's first year of school as an afterthought over coffee. Yes, I had to drive to the school within the hour to pick up registration materials.

I read through the registration in the parking lot and filled it out with a pen from the glove compartment. I never thought it would be like this. I was able to complete the generic portions — name, address, social security, doctor, allergies, but froze solid on the psychosocial section — an entire battery of questions that began: *Please list your child's strengths,* followed by *Now, please list the areas where your child may need extra help.* I've always had to fight my inclination toward being a smartass in school settings where individual characteristics are sorted out and graded like pieces of meat. Under "Strengths" I wanted to write, *He's a child.* Under "Weaknesses," *He lives in an adult's world.* Most of the questions seemed fair enough, but I couldn't get past the idea that anything I wrote could set up the expectations he'd have to live up to or the prejudices he'd have to live down. If I said he was brilliant, woe to him the weeks when he wasn't. If I said he could be trouble, he could be sent to the Gulag. Anything I thought of became dangerous in the wrong hands. I left psychosocial blank. A late application filled out by a father was already a red flag for trouble. I had nothing to lose. There was an interview scheduled for the following week; information about Casey's strengths and weaknesses was something I was more comfortable delivering by hand.

Susan picked up application materials for the private school where she works. After reading through the pages, she was struck by the same thing I was — Casey's birthday fell on the cutoff. From kindergarten to senior year, he would be either the youngest or the oldest in the class. The decision we made would set the course for the next thirteen years — maybe more. I thought Susan would know what we should do, being a teacher, but all her experience was in the middle-school years. For the primary years, she was about as lost as I was.

"How is a parent supposed to know?" I asked the public school counselor over the phone the next day.

"A parent knows their child better than anyone else," came the rote reply. I told her I appreciated that but had little idea about the workings of a kindergarten classroom. I told her we needed help. Casey could be a terror in a group setting. He was also reading. The woman said she'd be happy to discuss my "issues" during Casey's upcoming interview.

In the meantime, I called the local Montessori school to inquire about their approach and philosophy. I was told within the first minute of conversation about the five-thousand-dollar tuition and strict payment schedule. "We like to let people know about the fee up front as a system of weeding out unqualified candidates," the woman said. The system worked, although it wasn't the tuition that sent me running.

A week later, Casey and I had driven into the parking lot of the public school and sat down on two small plastic chairs to wait for our appointment with the counselor. Susan had taken the day off so that she and Owen could investigate a highly recommended alternative school that had a single opening left for the upcoming year and was having its last open house.

Casey was immediately interested in a rack of books. He moved his chair over and began going through them one by one. "He's reading?" the mother next to me asked with her jaw open. I told her he was but that it was something he'd picked up on his own. We hadn't pushed it. She didn't believe me.

"We're not sure if he's ready to start kindergarten yet," I said. "His birthday falls on the cutoff."

"But he's reading —" the woman said.

"Right, but wait till he spies the shiny blue ties on your daughter's pigtails. I can stop him from putting them into his pockets. I'm just not so sure anyone else can." The woman looked at him quietly paging through a book with few pictures and shook her head.

"He's reading," she said, as if I were some kind of idiot. "Look at him. He's ready."

So much for professional opinions.

"Children your son's age are not actually reading," the school counselor told me as we sat around a large table with Casey between us. She was a woman in her mid-fifties who looked as though she spent a majority of her time in a weight room. "They've memorized the way words look and they can identify them," she said, and pushed back the small yellow curls framing her taut, masculine face. "It's not actual reading. They're not actually sounding out new words."

Casey was sounding out every new word he could get his eyes on. I didn't push it. The woman already had me pegged for a show-off.

"Do you like to read, Casey?" she asked, her voice going artificially high. Casey shook his head. "No? . . . Daddy says that you *love* to read." He shook his head again. I looked at him and thought, *Don't hang me kid. Not here. Not now.* The woman scratched a note into what looked very much to be the beginning of the dreaded permanent file.

"Now here's what I'd like you to do," she said, putting a paper and pencil in front of him. She tugged the bottom of his chair to bring him closer to the table. "*Sit up, young man,*" she said. He startled and jerked to attention, the table at his chest. She gave him instructions, something about copying the images on the left into the boxes on the right, but I didn't actually hear it. I couldn't get past the "Sit up, young man."

Casey drew slowly on the paper. "While he's doing that," the woman said, "can you tell me about this section of the application that isn't filled out?"

"Sure. What would you like to know?"

"The questions here are pretty self-explanatory."

"Okay, the main thing is," I began, "my wife and I aren't sure that he's ready for school. His birthday falls on the cutoff."

"But you say he's reading."

"Yes. That's the whole problem —"

"Well, *reading* shouldn't be considered a problem, Mr. Parent."

"Right. Of course, I'm not saying *reading* is the problem —"

"I mean, if I saw a child this age actually *reading* —"

"Right — right — I know —"

"Although I'm not ready to agree with you that he is, in fact, *reading* —"

"The point is, we think he's more than ready to start school, academically speaking. Emotionally, we're not so sure."

"Your emotions, Mr. Parent, should not be the deciding factor here."

"*His* emotions — Casey's emotions. His level of maturity."

"Which doesn't necessarily have anything to do with you or your wife's emotions."

"Okay."

"Well, you're welcome to hold him until next year if you like. His birthday falls on the cutoff."

"Right — I know that." I waited a moment for her to give me more, the scratching of Casey's pencil between us was almost deafening.

"Is that what you'd like to do, then?" she asked, her voice going high as it did when she spoke to Casey.

"Well, that's the thing we're having trouble deciding," I said slowly. "That's what I hoped we could get some guidance on."

"Nobody else knows your child better than you, Mr. Parent."

"Okay. But is there some kind of assessment that might help us do the right thing?"

"This is your first child, isn't it?"

"Yes?"

She scratched another note into the file.

"Look," I said. "If he wasn't reading, we'd just hold him until next year. He can be a little rambunctious. On the other hand, we don't want him to be bored in preschool. And the studies on whether to start young or start older go back and forth."

"I spoke on the phone with you last week, didn't I?"

"Yes. I think it was you."

Another note.

"Well, let's look at what Casey has for us here," she said, pulling the paper out from under his pencil. His careful lines filled the page. For the most part, they had very little resemblance to the neat column of pictures on the opposite side. The woman glanced over each squiggle as though she was reading tea leaves. I waited for her to tell me what she saw, but she only wrote in the file. "Here's what we do," she said, snapping it shut. "We'll get a spot for Casey in one of our classrooms, you come to the orientation — see if your wife can make it. And we'll go from there. Okaaay?"

"That's it?"

"Everything else will be covered in the orientation. Okaaay?"

"And we decide when we're there if he's ready?"

"Yes, you can. I think the nurse is ready to see you now. Okaaay? It was very nice to meet you," she said with a handshake that helped me out of the chair, and then in the high voice, turning to Casey, "you too, young man!"

After a brief visit with a very overwhelmed school nurse, we were back in the car to make our way home. Casey had a thousand questions that he fired off from his car seat behind me. I did my best with them, and then we both fell silent to think about what had just happened. Along with the ringing "Okaaay?" I couldn't seem to shake the sound of the school counselor's *"Sit up, young man."* That one small demand resounded in me like nothing else she could have said. As I turned the truck onto the road that winds its way through Cherry Valley, I glanced over at Casey, gazing out his window at the rise and fall of passing hills. He was falling asleep. Then it hit me: young men don't fall asleep in their car seats. Young men go off to the prom and go off to college and go off to a first job. Casey was asleep with graham cracker crumbs around his mouth and a toy car in each tiny hand. The danger with a first child is that they get cast as the young man from the moment they're born. Every toy is for someone smaller, every behavior too childish — *Sit up, young man.* I'm a firstborn. I wasn't going to let it happen to him. Everything in its own time. Casey wasn't a young man yet. I didn't like the idea of anyone making him feel like he was.

"How'd it go?" Susan asked as I brought him in and laid him asleep on the couch. She was on the floor with Owen, who was circling her with a long line of Hot Wheels cars.

"Well, he's in," I said. "If we decide he's ready. I asked them to hold a spot for him to be on the safe side."

"How did he do? Was he good?"

"Yeah. Too good."

"He was too good?"

"They told him to sit up. The school counselor. At a table. She told him to 'Sit up, young man.'"

"And he did it?"

"Immediately."

"He listened," she said.

"Yeah. He listened. That's the part that killed me."

"Well, it's good if he listens, Marc."

"Sure, as long as he's being told something he should listen to. You'd have to have seen the look on his face when he shot to attention. He's not a 'young man' yet, Susan. You know? He's a kid. A *little* kid. And he wasn't slouching. He couldn't slouch if he tried — he's just a bundle of energy, he can barely bend his body to get his shoes on. He was sitting perfectly — he was comfortable. Now, why being comfortable would annoy a *school counselor* is beyond me."

"She probably didn't mean anything by it."

"This is the thing, Susan. It's not what anyone would say

to him that bothers me. She called him a 'young man' — big deal. He's been called that before, but never by someone who wanted him to *believe* it. It's what he believes that I'm worried about. He'll be called worse things than 'young man,' hopefully later in life when he's able to let it roll off. Right now he's wide open — anything anyone pours into him goes straight to the bottom, you know? He still believes it all. It's this agreement we've had going back and forth between us — we believe each other. It's all he knows. He believes us, we believe him. The only thing he knows is to believe."

"And that will have to change, Marc."

"I know it will. Isn't that a shame? I know . . . it has to. I'm trying not to be overprotective. I just don't think he's ready to sit up straight yet. That's all. Sitting up and all that goes along with it."

"I know what you're saying."

"So how was the visit to the highly touted alternative school?"

"Oh, it was terrific — an old farmhouse with lots of animals, a man about your age who takes the children for long walks through the woods, they climb trees and float little boats down the stream. Sound familiar?"

"Sounds familiar."

"Sounds very familiar."

"Not for us?"

"I had them reserve a spot to be on the safe side. We can cancel later if we need to. In the meantime we can pore over these," she said, handing me a stack of preschool brochures.

"Casey's appointment for the kindergarten at my school is tomorrow. Plan on about four hours. The teachers take him through a day of activities, and he's given a full battery of cognitive and behavioral tests by our staff psychologists. They tell me the kids usually love it." She gave me a thin smile. "I'll make sure to ask them not to tell Casey to sit up."

"Right," I said with a laugh. "His father doesn't allow it."

I glanced over the pamphlets Susan had given me — every place with a shingle to hang to call itself a preschool. There were lots of church schools, a few that looked interesting, many that didn't. A tumbling school, schools with pools, "learning centered" schools (as opposed to "ignorance centered" schools?), schools with cutesy names and others with serious names to suggest the highest of academic pursuits, even a school within proximity of a broken-down helicopter for the children to play on — the broken-down helicopter school — for discriminating parents who feel the morals and values of a broken-down helicopter have been lost in the fast pace of this modern world! I suddenly understood that a woman calling Casey a young man should be the least of my worries. This was not going to be easy.

"Hello, Casey!" the woman cooed. The words seemed to glow in her mouth. Casey looked excitedly around the classroom.

"Say hello, Casey," I said, trying to catch his attention. His eyes flew around me. The woman and I exchanged hellos. "This is a friend of Mama's," I said. "She's a teacher too.

You're going to stay with her for a few hours and then Owen and I will come back to pick you up."

"Hello, Casey," the teacher tried again. Casey glanced around her to a group of children sitting in a quiet circle at the far end of the room. A teacher in the middle of the circle read softly to them. The foyer we were in was bespeckled with clever crafts and decorations — very much the look of the very professional, very expensive private school. This was a tiptoe place. It was beautiful. The air was rose-colored with gentle softness. I should have known to turn and walk out right there.

"We've been looking forward to meeting you, Casey," the teacher said quietly with her eyes wide.

"Chip," Casey blurted with his eyebrows down. "My name is Chip."

I had no idea.

"Casey." I bent down, whispering to him. "Casey, this is a school. The teacher is going to use your real name today."

"Chip *is* my real name," he said, his face knotted with truculence.

"That's okay, dad," the teacher mouthed silently. I shook my head in disbelief. Casey turned and looked into the room like a teenager eyeing a pepperoni pizza. *He's going to eat them alive,* I thought, and the weightlifting counselor at the public school suddenly came to mind — a woman who knew how to beat a kid like Casey to the punch. *They're not going to tell him to sit up here,* I thought. *He's going to skin them first, and then he's going to eat them alive.*

"Go ahead and join the group, Casey," she said and suddenly corrected — *"Chip."* And he was off like a bowling ball to the pins. I couldn't watch. "He'll be fine," she said, touching my shoulder. "He's *adorable*."

I knew we were in trouble four hours later when Owen and I picked him up and the teacher walked toward us with his artwork in her hands — a coat hanger wrapped in tin-foil and covered with planets and stars — rockets and space shuttles hanging from orange yarn and large red letters in the middle that spelled out the name: C-H-I-P.

"Is this your daddy and brother, Chip?" the teacher asked. He looked past us. There was wildness behind his eyes. She introduced herself. It was the other teacher, who had been reading to the children when we came in. "He was *wonderful,*" she said. I looked again at little Chip. His mind was racing. He was looking out the window, talking quietly to himself. "He *really* was," the teacher went on. *I don't believe you,* I thought. *I think you're just being nice.* She, too, had put her hand on my shoulder — a conciliatory gesture that gave her away. I knew Casey too well. I knew from the look behind his eyes that he had been a wild wind through their peaceful classroom.

I crouched down to him as the teacher said hello to Owen. "Was it all right, Case?" I whispered. He leaned in for a hug, looking past the side of my head.

"Yeah, Daddy," he said softly. His voice was hoarse. I didn't believe him either.

Susan got the real story. When she returned from work that night, she laid it out for me. "Everybody loved him," she began. "The psychologist said she'd never met a child quite like him. I got to look at the tester's results. What they do is compare the scores of all the applicants and rank them.

Casey was one of the last ones, since we were so late to get him in — they were able to compare him to the whole group. In reading ability, he scored the highest."

"No surprise."

"Right."

"But don't forget — he's not actually reading," I said. "According to the experts, he's only looking at letter arrangements and figuring out what they say."

"This will surprise you," she went on. "He scored very close to the highest in math ability. It was something like — only two or three of the other kids scored higher."

"We haven't done a thing with math."

"I know — isn't it something? It's really surprising," she said. "I don't understand it. They say he loves to manipulate numbers and he's really good at it."

"Maybe it was Chip — he was channeling a boy genius from the middle of the country named Chip."

"Which brings me to the behavioral part of all this."

"Not as good."

"They have some kind of a test that's supposed to measure a child's frustration threshold."

"And?"

"He scored low on that."

"Frustrates easily."

"That's it."

"I guess that's no surprise either."

"And I have a feeling he was a little wild with the other kids."

"They said that?"

"In so many words, yes, they said that. They describe him as a very exciting child to teach. One of the testers wrote in her notes that she's never had a child try to negotiate her out of questions he couldn't answer — most kids give a wrong answer or just clam up."

"Not Case."

"Not Case — that's right. She describes him in her notes as 'precocious' — *adjective, characterized by unusually early development in mental aptitude.* I looked it up. I'd always associated the word with a brat."

"Right."

"It's not what it means, though. Everybody really liked him. They want him in the school, Marc. They want him in the preschool. Not the kindergarten."

"No kidding. Well, finally, someone to step out on a limb with this."

"They think he'd benefit from waiting a year."

"They do."

"But it's our decision. We can think about it. We'll get something official about all this in the mail. In the meantime, I've asked them to hold a spot in either class."

"Just to be on the safe side," I said.

"Just to be on the safe side," she said.

I spent the next week looking at preschools. Even though we hadn't decided he would go, I wanted to step inside a few just to see what was out there. With Owen on my hip and Casey's hand in mine, I did just that. The entirely predictable concern I had about each one I visited was that it wouldn't challenge Casey in a way that would keep him from becoming bored. For Casey, boredom has always been mayhem's spark. He never stays bored for very long before it sets in. But as far as I could make out, every preschool, no matter what they called themselves, was pretty heavy on shapes, colors, and seasons in the first half of the year. Even the "learning centered" schools would only talk about introducing the first letters of the alphabet after December.

As I was looking through all the area had to offer, Susan and I had also begun to canvass every friend, relative, and acquaintance who had ever navigated these waters. For the most part, the people who started their child early thought we should start Casey early. The ones who had waited thought we should have him wait. The arguments ran strong at either end, the two sides eventually canceling each other out. But in the course of all the back-and-forth, I became convinced of one thing — wherever we decided to send Casey for his first year of school, we would do our best to get him into a classroom where he didn't stick out in a positive or negative way, one where he wouldn't get used to hearing the teacher constantly say his name. A place that was neither excited nor perturbed by him. One that could keep up without passing him by. A place where he simply fit. The longer I looked, the clearer it became that despite the fact that he was old enough for kindergarten, despite the fact that he was reading, or something to that effect, Casey would get a better start in preschool.

We ruled out sending him to Susan's school, mostly because of the distance from our house. I was nearly settled on a church-affiliated school in town — a large, shining thing with a nice playground and a gymnasium with twenty trikes to tear around on during rainy days. "Big, old-fashioned trikes," I told Susan. "Can you imagine? Just like the kind we rode as kids!"

And then on my second visit, I'd come in a little early and caught the children returning to their classrooms from recess. Each of them, as they walked, held a tiny finger against the wall. Then a little later, a girl by herself on the way to the bathroom and then a very young boy walking glumly down the long hall to wait for his mother in the office — both of them dragging a finger against the wall.

"Can I ask you a stupid question?" I said to the secretary. She looked up suspiciously. "Why do the children drag their fingers against the walls?"

"Oh — that," she said, letting her shoulders down.

"Is that a stupid question? I've just been standing here trying to figure it out."

"No, not really," she said. "It's to keep them in control. We had a kid fall two years ago."

And all I could think was, *You had a kid fall two years ago??!! Just one kid?*

"Was the kid hurt?" I asked.

"*No* — thank God," she said, rolling her eyes. "He was okay. Just a bump."

"And ever since that bump . . ." I said. She smiled and nodded. "You've had the children do that with the wall."

"And there hasn't been another incident."

Not counting calluses?

The school's director and architect of the finger-to-the-wall came to show me through the classrooms. As she brought me around, I suddenly saw the neat rows of toys and tidy circles of chairs in a whole new light. What had so impressed me on my first visit had soured now that I knew the cost of this order. I had been naive, never thinking about what I'd have to actually do to my boys to keep our house as neat. The idea of Casey spending a year with his finger to a cinder-block wall made the whole sit-up-young-man business seem like a silly Mary Poppins game. In one classroom, a smartly dressed teacher with brightly dyed red hair and ruler-straight bangs took us through the steps of an elaborate time-out procedure — the kind of thing that could set a child up for a lifetime of fetishes. I finished the tour, thanked the director very much, told her to release our reservation, and walked the guys out to the truck, dizzy with the thought that I had almost chosen Casey's first school on the basis of a nice collection of trikes.

"This proves it," I told Susan that night. "I do not know what I'm doing. I was about to write a check to this place."

"But you didn't."

"Right, but I almost did — I almost had us sending him there."

"Yes, but you didn't and we're not. I'm not worried. We'll get him in the place that's right."

"Well, I'd love to know why you think that, because I thought I had a pretty good handle on all this and then I turn around to discover I'm a complete amateur. I was seduced by a line of trikes. What does that say?"

"It says you can appreciate a sturdy, well-built trike —"

"Please —"

"— It says you know your son, Marc, you know how much he'd love to scream around a gym floor on that thing. It says you want him in a place that he can hardly wait to go to every morning. There is nothing wrong with that. I am not worried. We will find the perfect place."

"Why do you think so?"

"I know you won't settle for anything less."

"Are we putting too much on this?"

"No, we're not."

"A lot of people just send their children to the place closest to them — probably works out just fine most of the time."

"I don't think we're putting too much on this."

"Because I don't like any of the places I've seen. We've reserved a spot in practically every school in town — it's getting ridiculous. You'd think one of them would be right."

"There's one more."

"One more!"

"Right here in the valley. I made an appointment for us to look at it this weekend."

"Right here in the valley?"

"The little stone church by the sandwich shop. There is a school on the side of it. I just heard that it has the highest rating in the district."

"Why didn't we look at it first?"

"Oh, I don't know — maybe because it was standing right in front of us. Maybe because it was here in our backyard all along."

Another church school. Given the staunch law and order of the last one I'd visited, I was wary of what I'd find at this one. We drove into the small parking lot entrance marked with a carved wooden sign that read Cometh. A sign at the other end read Goeth. Across the road, along the circle drive at the front of the school were similar signs to guide traffic — a Yea at one end, a Nay at the other. For me, it was a good start. When it comes to religious humor, it's always the thought that counts. As a kid, one of my favorite priests used to tell a joke at the end of every mass that always got a huge laugh even though he'd rattle through it so fast you could only hear half of it. It was the attempt that got everybody going. He was trying. People would start laughing as the joke began — it didn't matter what he was saying by the end of it. Someone in this place was trying too.

"Who's meeting us here?" I asked Susan as we whisked the boys across the road.

"The director — I spoke with her yesterday on the phone. She told me they're already full."

"Why is she seeing us if they're already full?"

"We're on a waiting list."

"Daddy — what does *cometh* mean?" Casey asked as we jogged past the sign.

"Not reading," Susan said.

"Definitely not reading," I said.

We approached the building to the sound of a chorus. The front doors burst open and a group of young teenage boys and girls came tumbling out. They ran around us, laughing and teasing with each other. Two of the girls stopped to

flirt with Casey. The sound of singing filled the air. Susan
ran ahead to catch the door. I pulled Casey along, the four of
us stepped inside, and for a moment we just stood still. To
our right was a group of about thirty children aged seven to
fifteen, singing at the top of their lungs. A madly enthusias-
tic woman led the group through the words as she jumped
around in a grand pantomime. The man playing the piano
next to her was bouncing off his stool. A large room directly
ahead of us looked like command central for the Mardi
Gras parade — projects of every kind, all in various stages
of completion, covered the floor in a rainbow of colors. Children of every age milled about, cutting here, gluing there.
At the back of the room, a group of adults were preparing a
feast in a large open kitchen. To our left in what looked like
an office, another group worked over a large mural that was
spread over several desks. Susan shouted over the roar of the
chorus to several of the people inside, asking if anyone had
seen the director of the preschool.

"That's me!" a woman shouted back and walked toward
us with a big smile. In her hands, she held together the skull
and backbone of a dinosaur model. "I'm director of the
school and gluer of the bones." Susan introduced herself and
the boys and me. The woman smiled and nodded. "I'd
shake your hand," she yelled over the din and then held up
the model, "but I'm having an archeological moment — the
kids will kill me if I let this thing fall apart. It's almost dry."

I made a lame joke about most museum dinosaurs being
assembled by preschool directors. She laughed, although I
don't think she heard what I said. Another group of teenagers

came whipping around us. *"Whoa,"* she said, lifting the bones to keep them from being hit. "Let's go someplace a little quieter — we're just starting the first week of several of our summer camps. You wanted to see some of the classrooms right? Follow me."

The rooms, although empty, were every bit as filled with the evidence of frenzied activity. And not a neat lineup of trikes in sight. Not a single pristine toy or book or block or desktop to be found — just one organized mess after another. A lot like our house. This was a building that had seen the likes of many Caseys. As we walked through, Susan and I peppered the director with every question we could think of. By the time we finished the tour, I realized that I'd been in love with the place from the moment we stepped inside.

"We cover all basic academic requirements," the director said as she wound things up. "But the school's main goals are to teach kindness and to build self-esteem. The biggest thing we want is for a child like Casey to look forward to coming here — to see school as an exciting, interactive, positive place to learn."

"Perfect," Susan said to herself.

"That's great," I said.

"We think it is," she said, bouncing her eyebrows at Casey. He smiled and looked away.

"Now what about 'time-outs'?" I asked.

"What about them?" she said as she turned and slowly set the bones on a shelf.

"How do they work here?"

"They don't," she said. "We don't believe in time-outs. Especially at Casey's age."

"So what do you do with a child who's being impossible?"

"Head him off at the pass," she said with a smile. "Stop him before he gets there."

"But if he does get there? What do you do then?"

"You can almost always redirect a child out of an undesirable behavior. It's just that it takes a little more work than issuing a time-out. We have a lot of tricks. Here, look — this is one we call the shaving-cream table," she said pointing to a low plastic tub on legs. "We've found that it's pretty tough for a four- or five-year-old to hold on to a bad attitude in front of a whole mound of shaving cream. So when your child comes home smelling like Brut, you'll know it's because he's been acting like one!"

A group of young girls came running into the room to say that at least six people were looking for her.

"Tell everyone I'm almost finished here," she said. The girls ran out.

"So, we're on the list then?" I asked.

"Well, no. Not if you don't want to be. We had a cancellation this morning."

"*You have an opening?*" Susan asked. The director nodded.

"*Can we reserve the spot?*" I asked reflexively.

"We aren't taking reservations at this point," she said. "There are people on the list behind you."

"Well, . . . can we give you a deposit then?" I asked.

"We don't take deposits. Would you like to send Casey to our school this fall?" I looked to Susan — straight into her eyes and her I-told-you-so smile. *I knew we'd find the perfect place.*

"Yes," I said, turning back to the director. "Yes, we would."

"Come with me and I'll get you the papers. You can send the check for the first month in the mail. Welcome aboard, Casey," she said and then got right down into his face. *"You're gonna like it here."*

The summer slipped away as summers always do — lost somewhere between the beer and the barbecue. A couple of nights on your back staring into the stars, a few casts, a couple of laughs, a ball game, a midnight swim if you're lucky, and then it's gone. The first meeting of Casey's class was on a hot, late-August night. Regular classes would begin in September. The purpose of tonight's gathering was to meet the teachers and talk about what the coming year would bring.

We had assembled in the Mardi Gras room, which had taken on a more serious tone now that the colorful ribbons of papier-mâché and metallic streamers had been replaced by rows of metal chairs. Teachers and administrators sat behind a long table next to a podium at the front of the group. It felt like a graduation ceremony and in a way, it was — but for parents, not children. I looked around the room at the moms and dads sitting on either side of their child. We had all made it. Our children were ready for the next step. None had succumbed to illness, none were dropped or shaken, none taken by a drunk driver or stray bottle of medicine. Electrical outlets had been covered for the last five years, pan handles turned in, car seats buckled, swimming pool gates locked, hands held tight, strange dogs kept at bay. Thanks to equal measures of skill, determination, and luck, we had all made it to graduation.

Susan and I scanned the faces of the teachers, trying to guess which one was ours. Before we could decide, the director stood up and identified each of them. After the introductions, Casey's teacher walked up to the podium to deliver a prepared welcome speech. Her face was wrapped with a nervous calm — the kind that brings out the monotone in the best of us.

"This is her least favorite part of the job," I whispered, "talking to a group of parents over a microphone."

"She hates it," Susan agreed.

If you only knew how nervous we all are, I thought. *How hopeful we are that you will be kind, that this isn't something you've grown tired of doing, that our children will soar with you and not in spite of you, that they will still believe it all when you're done with them — that you will let that be true in their world for this one last year. You could never know how much we hope that you will please, please — to the very depth of all the word means — please, be kind.*

She read carefully through her piece as if the words would break like dishes if delivered with too much inflection — something about being eager for the coming year and the privilege of spending it with our children. Very nice. She ended with a short prayer and then click-clacked on tall, wide heels back to her seat.

"Well, that should be a bright spot in your day," Susan whispered.

"What?"

"Casey's teacher."

". . . Yeah?"

"She's a babe."

"I wasn't gonna say it," I said.

Later in the evening, we were divided up into individual classrooms with the actual kids and parents we'd be spending the year with. It was a fresh-looking group. Each child had a mother and a father who seemed to be enjoying each other's company — the nation's divorce rate not yet reflected in the preschool years. There was no talk of learning disabilities or behavioral disorders, no one commiserating over the ravages of bulimia or depression. No one worried about cigarettes or drugs or promiscuity or even a class bully. No one was having trouble with math. There were no weak tennis players. No sloppy handwriters and no bad spellers. No jocks or nerds or stoners or brains and not a single tone-deaf child in the room.

Casey's teacher handed out cookies, and we all ate them as our kids hurled toys and books off the shelves. After taking us through the paces of a typical day, she asked if there were any questions. No one spoke up. When there are so many, it's hard to pick just one. Finally, as a way to fill the void, a man asked about field trips. There would be many, she said, and we all nodded because field trips are almost always good. Then a woman who told everyone her son was allergic to peanuts. We all nodded again and then shook our heads because peanuts are in just about everything.

Later on, before leaving, we walked over to introduce Casey to the teacher and then say good night. "Hey, kiddo!" she cheered and held out a hand. "Gimme five, bud." Casey slapped hard. She didn't flinch. I liked that. "Anything I need to know about him?" she asked.

"Nothing you won't find out in the first five minutes alone with him," Susan said.

"My kinda guy."

"So, I'll be the one," I said awkwardly. "I'm gonna be — I'm the dad — I'm going to be the one picking him up every day, so . . . it'll be me that's getting him . . . as opposed to the mother."

"That's fine," she said.

"Sure, sure — not that it's really that important, I guess."

"Marc's just telling you so your jaw doesn't drop open every day when he comes in to pick him up," Susan said and they both had a laugh.

For the drive home, Casey was mostly quiet as we peppered him with our positive spin on the night. That's your school! That's your classroom! That's your teacher! She seems nice! It looks fun there! What a cool place! The kids were nice too! — and on and on. Plain and simple nerves. After we calmed down a little, I finally invited him to tell us what he thought of the night.

"What do you make of all that, Case?" I asked, glancing into the backseat. He was leaning against the window, staring out at the stars. "What did you think about that place? . . . Casey?"

". . . Good," he said.

"You thought it was good, honey?" Susan asked. I glanced back again. He was still looking out at the stars, nodding. Good. It was good.

I'll try to remember that as you head off, I thought, looking into the same stars — *as you begin this journey away from us. Good. Even when the destination leaves us without you. Good. Even though I don't feel it. Not at all. Good. I know it is. Good.*

But I can only say the word.

———

"Casey's clothes are on top of the dresser," Susan says as I walk through the door. "The red shirt you like him in and his new jeans. Where were you?"

"Just up by the barn," I say, kicking off my boots.

"Have you been up there long?"

"I walked up early. I couldn't sleep."

"His 101 Dalmatians sneakers are on the porch. They're mostly red, so they'll match the shirt. That should be okay."

"You didn't have to do —"

"I couldn't sleep either. I know I didn't have to do that — do you want a pancake?"

"No, thanks."

"The boys just finished theirs, so they should be okay. Casey gets a snack at school," she says on the sudden verge of tears. "But he'll be hungry when you pick him up."

"Okay, Suz."

"Make sure to bring something in case he's hungry. There's cheese right here in the bottom of the fridge. Look, I'll just leave it out."

"That's fine."

"A new box of graham crackers in the pantry, these apples are good."

"I know, Susan," I say, trying to slow her down.

"He hasn't had an apple in a couple of days. Owen, would you like another pancake?" He nods even though his mouth is full and there's one on his plate. "I think I have time to make one more. *Casey!*" she shouts.

"*No, mama!*" he shouts from the other room.

"*I'm making you one more,*" she calls back and then looks to me. "Give it to the dog if he doesn't eat it."

The cruel irony of Susan's job is that after years of being present for hundreds of children on their first day of school, she's not able to be there for her own. Casey's first day falls on the same day as hers. Of all the times she could take off, the first day of school is not one of them.

"*Come and eat this, Casey,*" she shouts, putting the pancake onto his plate.

"*I don't want it, Mama,*" he shouts back.

"Here, Owen," she says, tossing it onto his plate. "You can eat Casey's. Here's yours too."

"Suz —"

"*Just give them to the dog, Marc.*"

"Yup."

"*Look at the time* — I have to go. *Casey* —" He comes sliding around the corner in his pajamas and falls into her arms. They hold each other tight. She dries her eyes with his head squeezed to her shoulder so he won't see the tears. "I don't know what these are all about," she says to herself. "I didn't expect to be like this . . . I just wish I could be there." She dries her eyes again and pulls his face right up to hers. "I want you to have a really good first day of school," she says. "I'm going to be thinking about you all day." And then, nose to nose, she closes her eyes and tells him she loves him. He reaches both arms around her neck and gives a long squeeze.

"Mama?" he asks softly in her ear.

"Yes, Case?"

"Do I have to eat the pancake?"

"You can give it to the dog, honey," she says rising to go. She gives Owen a kiss and grabs her keys off the shelf. "The camera," she says, pointing to it.

"You bet," I say. And she pauses for a moment in the open doorway.

"It feels like the end of something," she says, her nose wrinkling, the tears coming back.

"I'll have a cake when you get home, babe."

"I don't need a cake, Marc."

"Sure you do. We'll eat the whole damn thing for supper." The boys cheer. "There, it's set in stone. You can give your piece to the dog." She waves me off as she turns out the door. *"If he's not full of pancakes,"* I call after her.

After dressing Casey, I tell him to stand still. I take a picture. I run ahead of him as he steps out of the front door. I turn around. "Just wait, Case — back up a little," I say. "Stand still." I take a picture. With Owen on my hip, I take a picture of him in front of the school. Then another one when he's not turning his head. "Stand still, Case," I say. "Stand still — back up a little." *Click.* In the classroom. "Look again, Casey — stand still, stand still." Stand still, stand still. Back up — even better. Keep going. All the way back. Let's do the whole thing over again, starting say, at around three months. It was great when you were three months old. Let's back all the way to three months and then just stand still so I can toss this stupid little camera into the road.

"Gimme five, Casey!" The teacher says, scooting up to him with her hand out. He slaps hard. She doesn't flinch.

"Don't tell me you remember everyone's names," I say.

"Just the kids," she says, like it isn't much. "Just the kids."

"Then I'll wait a few weeks before telling you mine."

"I would really appreciate that," she says with a good laugh.

"So I'm not sure how he's going to take this," I say. "We've talked about it. He seems excited."

"You can wait in the hall after you leave," she says, her eyes suddenly serious. "If he does cry, it shouldn't be for long — listen and you'll see. I have an assistant and the director here to help me. As soon as parents leave, I get *really fun*. It's all about distractions at this age."

"I'm by the phone," I say. "And I live right down the road. Please, I want you to call me if he's having a hard time."

She looks at him unloading a bin of dinosaurs and flopping to his belly to push them around. "My guess —" she says, and then watches a little longer "— my instinct tells me he'll be okay. I think so. You can tell sometimes."

The other parents and younger siblings fill the room, and then begin to thin out as they slowly leave. There are tears, but not as many as there could be. The teacher, her assistant, and the school's director make a remarkable team. Their smooth handling of even the most panic-stricken children gives me the confidence I need to leave myself.

"Casey," I say. He comes over and leans into me. He knows what comes next. "I'm going to leave you now." His eyes puzzle and shoot up to the ceiling. His lip pops out. I feel the same way. "But I'll come back. This is a good place. I'll come back. I promise."

"Daddy?"

"What?"

"Is a promise is a promise?"

"Yes, Case."

"Is it?"

"A promise is a promise," I say. He leans into me again. I scoop Owen off the floor and pry a small car out of his hand. I give Casey a big hug, waving his teacher over as I do. *"You can start being really fun now,"* I mouth silently over his shoulder.

"Casey," she says, her voice like the booming sound of the entire world that would beckon him away. It echoes through my head and then goes deeper. I hold tight to Owen as Casey begins to pull away — thank God for second children. "Casey," she says again and he looks to her. "C'mere, kiddo. I want to show you something." She takes his hand and walks him off. She is very pretty. Susan was right. Very easy for a child to be drawn to. Her clothes are bright and colorful — a walking candy land, every inch from spangled boot to her long-flowing hair, fine-tuned to the desires of a child. "Have you ever seen what it's like —" she says, and glances back to give me an assuring nod and wave me out — "have you ever seen what it's like, Casey, to take *a whole can of shaving cream . . .*"

Owen rides my hip out the classroom door, a little unsure of why Casey's staying but grateful to be the one who's going with me. I listen by the wall for the sound of crying. There is none. And then I go.

So this is it.

This is the final piece of love. It's just as everyone has said. It's not complete until you let it go. Love grows bigger as you loosen your grip, because only as it floats away do you begin to see what it really is. Then it grows, not like a delicate rose but like the hardiest weed, sending its shoots out all around you.

I feel it happening. Walking from the school. Driving away. Home with Owen and Casey not with us. I'm an arm's length from the phone, the keys are still in the truck, but he's gone no matter how fast I can get back to him. This is the other side of what love is. The other side of the head-spinning joy of having him around. My head is still spinning — not from his presence now, but from the aftermath of that presence, the impression it's made in me. Like the hollow that's left when the stone is pulled from the ground, you only see what the stone has meant when the stone is taken away.

Absence is the piece that makes love whole. I never knew it until this moment, staring down into the hollow that's left in me now that he's gone. It doesn't feel good. It only feels right. And I'll tell him here so he will always know it. I'll tell Casey and Owen both, so we all remember this thing they've taught me: Love is a weed. Don't ever let anyone tell you it's a rose. Love grows wild. It flourishes where it's trampled. It multiplies where it's ripped from the ground. Its roots grow deeper through the suffering. I tell you this, my boys, only because it's true — I felt my strength when you pushed me to the breaking. I loved you more on the days you nearly killed me.

THE BRIGHTEST MOON

Tonight is the winter solstice, the year's longest night. The weathermen have just told me so. I jump up to look on the calendar because so much of what weathermen say is in doubt. I scan all the way down the month of December until I find the words written in small letters on the bottom of the twenty-first day — winter solstice. Right this time.

But there is more to this day than a winter solstice to get the local weathermen excited about staying up late. This year, the moon has conspired to make the solstice unique. Tonight is the full moon — not just any full moon, but the last one of the millennium. On top of that, it's also the closest it has been to the earth in the last one hundred and twenty-eight years. This is the part that gets weathermen giddy. Around here, anyway. "Drive without your headlights!" crows one. "And if we get a little reflective snow cover by then," says another, "*whoa* — step out at midnight and don't forget the sunglasses!"

We should all set the alarm clock and take a look after midnight, they say, when the moon is at its apex. I don't need to set the alarm clock. I'm usually up in this barn listening to muffled country music, the whir of the fan over the heater and the clicking sound of this keypad. Tonight it's the same.

"Don't forget to look at the moon," Susan said as I headed out. "On my drive home, the weatherman on the radio said it would really be something."

"Well," I said, putting on a cap and tucking my computer under my arm, "I wouldn't necessarily put too much on that. Weathermen on the whole are a pretty excitable bunch."

In the barn, I sit on the couch and listen to the radio while the room heats up. The latest country-music sensation is trying her luck at the old Eagles tune "Desperado." Seems it's practically a required element of the country music industry, as it churns out stars like loaves of bread — the rhinestone jacket deal-makers grilling every fresh face off the bus in Nashville — *You're cute, but how's your "Desperado"?* This girl is fine. She doesn't seem to have the first idea about what the words mean but has a voice like a bird. I'll listen to almost anyone sing "Desperado" and find something to like about it.

I turn the dial down to the NPR station. Someone is interviewing an astronomer about tonight's moon. He seems a little put off by all the excitement, in a way most astronomers are about the public's myopic fascination with the small pocket of the cosmos that can be seen by the naked eye. You can hear his annoyance with the once-in-a-lifetime hype when a simple backyard telescope will reveal once-in-a-life-time events on a weekly basis. "Looking up at tonight's moon," he says, "will be like looking into an overhead lamp of eighty watts as opposed to the usual sixty." Thanks so much. Astronomers on the whole: not an excitable bunch.

I'm into the middle of a difficult paragraph by the time midnight rolls around. I've momentarily forgotten about the moon. Then I have to stand up and walk away from a mash of sentences that refuse to come together. I throw on my hat and jacket and slip on my boots. I step out of the room into the darkness of the barn and walk up to the mas-sive door, grasping the handle and hauling it back with my full weight. The wheels groan against the top rail, the door rolls back like a giant wooden curtain, and the moon comes suddenly crashing down around me. For a moment, I stand frozen in the glow. Every familiar thing is new in this silver light. Nothing is the same as it was. I can see all the way out to the far side of the valley. At midnight. This brightest moon has changed it all.

I step out and walk across the ash-white ground to the banks of the black, glittering stream. Then, around the back of the barn, I gaze up the long planks stretching straight into a sky that is neither day nor night — each breath lifting from me like a blue spirit through the cold air. Time and space slowly reveal themselves and then become so incom-prehensibly endless that they freeze the imagination. I am changed by this light too.

As I stand with my head up and my eyes closed, my mind clear of all distractions, I can sense a passage. Casey has been in school for the past four months, and the days are different. We opened the door to let him out and the world came rushing in. Susan knows it too. Even Owen is affected. I don't know what it means. I only feel the change. I could spend the rest of my life thinking about what this time alone with them has meant, but it wouldn't change the fact that it's suddenly over.

The coming new year is only a few days away, the air is thick with retrospect and uncertainty. But the future will always be uncertain. So it is with Casey and Owen. I'm too aware of what is left behind to look forward to the unknown of what will be. I can't imagine another time as rich as this. I can only hope and wait for it to come. But I will move forward as I'm waiting, always holding to this thing they have given me in these first years, this brilliant light that will guide me through the dark nights of this life, the daring grace of this silvery dusk that will show me the way.

I never thought that I might already know the ones who could shed light into life's biggest questions, that I might be wiping their noses and begging them to keep the bathwater in the tub. I never thought I would lean in to hear the answers only to discover that they are revealed without the utterance of a single word. I never thought I would have to crouch down for the lessons. I never thought the greatest teacher I could ever hope to discover was a child.

From the day they were born, Casey and Owen have looked into my eyes to find their answers. My promise to the two of them is this — as you have believed in the things I have told you, I will believe in the things you have shown me. My promise is to never stop looking for your light. When it shines on me, I will know it is true. When it shines on me I will believe it all.

I turn from the barn and look to an opening in the woods — the path glowing like a once-in-a-lifetime invitation from this burning solstice moon. If there was ever a night to walk alone into the middle of the forest, this is the night. Just before I do, I stop at the tree line to look up one more time and think of what a comfort it is — how utterly decent that this longest night would also be the brightest.

ACKNOWLEDGMENTS

I am deeply grateful for the gift of family and friends who have supported me in obvious ways as well as in ways they will never know: my parents, Kevin and Maxine; my agent, David Black, who was the first to believe it all; Walter Bode, who walked me through the fire with a strong, gentle hand when this book was only notes on paper; Anna Quindlen, who was the first, after my mother and my wife, to call me a writer and is one of my favorite women to this day because of it; brothers and sisters, always dear, Brodie, Ted, Aimee, and Denise; Tom and Delores Hawe; Joseph Murphy; Kevin Confoy and Jodi Wright; Steve Alden; James MacDonald and Karen Rizzo; Frank Clem and Barbara Bloom; Paul and Maddalena Skemp; Lisa and Charlie Cohan; Dick and Clare Donovan and family; Ken and Joanne Davis; at Black Inc., Joy Tutela, Susan Raihofer, and Gary Morris; at Little, Brown, my editors Sarah Burnes and Michael Pietsch, also Judy Clain,

Heather Rizzo, Beryl Needham, Linda Biagi, Kelly Blair, Claire Smith, and Betty Power; and finally, dearest Susan, who has given me the greatest gift of all — those boys, oh those beautiful, beautiful boys, who are so very much like their mother.

My thanks, my love.

Marc Parent is the author of *Turning Stones: My Days and Nights with Children at Risk* and has written for the *New York Times* and *USA Today* among other publications. He lives in rural Pennsylvania with his wife and two sons.

Author photo by Rob Kinmonth